INTO
DEPRESSION
AND BEYOND

JOHN COX

PublishAmerica
Baltimore

First printing

Cover photograph: The author photographed this sunset in Israel during a six-week study-tour. It was taken from the Eastern shore of the Sea of Galilee as the sun set over the hills behind Tiberias, and in the direction of Nazareth (the birthplace of the Son who rose for all eternity – and in Whom there is no darkness).

ISBN: 1-59286-869-X
PUBLISHED BY PUBLISHAMERICA, LLLP
www.publishamerica.com
Baltimore

Printed in the United States of America

I would like to acknowledge and thank the many people who have supported, cared for, befriended, and encouraged me through the difficult years described in these pages. To name those of whom I am aware would inevitably result in my omitting others unwittingly, such as the many who have diligently prayed for my healing. You know who you all are and I extend a sincere and profound 'thank you' to you.

I dedicate this book to my two lovely daughters Carmen and Michelle, who have loved me despite being hurt by some of my actions. They continue to bless me and give me hope, pride, love, purpose and a joy far beyond their comprehension.

I also thank God for His mercy and strange faithfulness; we still have much to talk about….

Contents

Foreword

This collection of poems spans a period of nearly 7 years and provides an autobiographical reflection of a harrowing journey through depression and 'mid-life transition'. The core group of poems (from *Dead Man Writing* to *Thank God for Friends)* was written sequentially during the most intense period of a decline into depression that lasted for approximately four months. The dark times then concertinaed through various shades of melancholy and turmoil for years after that.

Reflecting on these writings, I observed that many of the poems that spoke of hope only really began to become true for me about two years after they had been written. Certainly the slowness of progress took me by surprise and there were many false starts along the way. Part One (Flickerings) deals with the core journey of depression while Part Two (Rekindled) articulates and reflects on the wider context surrounding the experience – including the attitudes and reactions of others (from my hyper-sensitive perspective at the time).

I included the prose because they reference themes underlying some of the significant strands informing my understanding of the turmoil. Those themes invariably can be traced back to childhood and issues relating to the nuclear family. In my case that is also interwoven with my journey as a Christian and my adventures within the established church.

I am also very aware that I am no expert in the psychology or treatment of depression; consequently my writings and expressed opinions are purely subjective observations. If this material is useful, I am of course interested to receive feedback and I would be delighted to hear from you (email: johncox@shaw.ca).

FLICKERINGS
(PART ONE)

A bruised reed He will not break and a flickering flame He will not snuff out.

(Isaiah 42:3)

Overwhelmed

I never anticipated the crash.

Its rumblings began a long time ago....

Newly born, gurgling from a spring in the highland mountains, an adolescent bouncing over boulders, rocks and cliffs, slowly maturing to wind through an infinitely varied terrain, and eventually draining into the vast ocean at 'death' – such is life. Along the route many tributaries splice the main stream like veins pouring all manner of material into the life-cycle flow.

In this analogy of life the various tributaries drain a multitude of terrains inhabited by family, parents, siblings, friends, marriage, faith, education, work … etc. Many enhance, some make little difference, and others are extremely significant. On occasion, the impact of a particular rivulet or raging stream is only fully comprehended years later, maybe way downstream, maybe never.

Neither is everything that flows within our river of life necessarily pure and refreshing, life giving or stimulating. In my life, those meltdown months of depression were an experience of turmoil, emotional breakdown, guilt, anger, confusion, questioning, doubt, and pain. It was as if a major deluge in the mountains caused every tributary of my life, past and present, to gush forth in a flood that, unlike Noah, I had neither anticipated nor prepared for.

In vain I tried to sandbag the hemorrhaging, but no resources within me could withstand the force. Eventually the waters breached my banks and I waited out the ensuing flood praying for the turbulence to subside. For those who knew me and inhabited one of the shores of my being it was understandably tempting to suggest that 'this is what the "issue" is', or 'that is what caused the flood'. They may have been right. But I, standing in the silt and debris surveying the damage, could only reply, "Yes, possibly; but not just that, I don't comprehend the intensity of all of this."

As in any time of crisis, deep character strengths and flaws are revealed together with hidden fears and longings. There were times when the place was so dark that I could understand why some would choose suicide as an option (even fleetingly), and why for others turning to medication, drugs, or even frantic activity, is a desperate response attempting to dull the pain and shrink the demons. These are neither logical nor rational places; and I certainly had never fully comprehended the potency and raw power of despair, depression, and hopelessness. Neither did I appreciate how incredibly vulnerable it feels to be the flickering flame or the bruised reed, totally at the mercy of others and deeply sensitive to every response and reaction shown.

I thirsted for hope and it was a long time coming.

depression is a living hell
dark
overwhelming
hopelessly helpless
every adjective conjured up
hardly communicates the galactic void
of infinite aloneness at the epicentre
of such a black and unholy space

I met a man recently
who had survived a similar journey
he told me that for him
a clip in the movie *A Perfect Storm*
most eloquently expressed his despair
and sense of helpless hopelessness

the scene he described takes place
after the fishing boat
has disappeared beneath the waves
one man swims alone on the surface
huge gray waves roll under heavy black skies
a strong wind blows and the rain pours down around him
the camera-lens sweeps over the sea
and there is nothing else in sight
finally it pauses framing the solitary figure
silently magnifying his absolute vulnerability
then gradually the camera pans back
and he becomes smaller and smaller until he is lost
disappearing amidst the vastness
of the stormy hostile environment in which he is trapped
there's no hope of rescue
no one sees or hears him
we know and he knows
that before long
he will sink forever
one thing is certain
he will not survive
on his own

I'm not there now

I'm not there now

caught
paralyzed
sinking into quicksand
sucked down by despair
gasping for air
grabbing for straws
snatching for hope....

I'm not there now

dancing on streets paved with gold
radiant with joy
laughing through music-filled days
where sorrow is healed
and every tear
at last
at last is wiped away

I'm somewhere
in-between
and it's here we meet
you and I
incomplete

In the Shadow of Death

Walking through the Valley of the Shadow of Death, or perhaps it would be more apt to say, 'surviving the journey', is a miracle in itself. Those who have travelled this tortuous path are only too well aware of the many moments when one wonders if there will ever be an end to the hellish nightmare. "Down there" I never imagined the dawning of a day when I would sit and reflect and write about where I *had been*. I could not conceive of a time when the pain and darkness would lift sufficiently to permit such a luxurious possibility.

I have had the privilege of counseling (listening to) hurting people for more than fifteen years and have walked alongside others as they have navigated their painfully slow pace through similar valleys. While I thought I understood what I was hearing I could neither see nor comprehend the pain of every step, like a bare foot pressed down on sharp thorns and stones. I gave advice, I threw lifelines, I quoted phrases and I encouraged choices ... but with the best will in the world I had no idea ... it could be quite so bleak, so empty, so lonely, so painful, so unbelievably God-forsaken!

My purpose in writing is to attempt to give expression to portions of this journey of anguish and survival, primarily for those who are presently enduring such a place. When I reread this 'stuff' I am very tempted to walk away and leave it as my private record of an awful time. But there are also those who very much want to 'be there for one whom they love and care about' and don't understand what is going on, or what they can do to be 'helpful'.

In the midst of my darkness I longed to read more that would articulate something of what I was feeling and also provide me with a glimmer of hope for the future. Maybe a few of these words will offer some hope where hope is presently not visible at all. The hope of which I speak is not articulated only with spoken or written words but in the deep affirmation of the broken person. It is communicated through simple acts of kindness over a long period of time: walks, cups of coffee, a phone call; and through the love of friendship that patiently, quietly, consistently and repeatedly affirms the truth:

"I believe in you. ... I love you, even as you despair of yourself. I will wait with you and walk with you for as long as it takes. I don't know how long that will be for you but I do know that it will not be forever. When you are ready you can talk ... if you'd like to ... with me or with someone else. I will do my best to listen without judgement or argument. Although I cannot comprehend where you are right now, I can at least understand that whatever the source of your pain and anguish, there is a real and genuine hurt within you, which for now needs to be allowed to be. There will be a time when this too will end and I'm committed to walking by your side, at your own pace, toward that day one step at a time."

Living Underground

for a very long time
through many summers
winters
and season changes
the surface was barren
sun-baked
sometimes soaked in rain
still dead quiet
an eternal hide and no speak
human earth being

from time to time green wisps
protruded to bask in warmth
and in the fall ancient leaves
dropped from crooked fingers
like broken promises
unable to hang on anymore
relinquishing hope
their fetal forms
twirled lightly down
becoming ghosts that rustled
above the ground
tumbled by the breeze
before crumbling to dust

one day a gardener broke the crust
turning the soil for air and light to filter in
soaking the dormant roots
and nourishing the seeds
that no one knew about

except you
and he who 'had a suspicion'
that there was more down there in you
than met the eye

and after tilling and caring
painful cracks split shells long forgotten
sprouting shoots
that tentatively took root
t'was strange to feel such life stir within

but it's easier to lie fallow
no one troubles to dig and hoe
or pierce the dirt disturbing the status quo

let me be
was the frightened plea
while still yearning for the smell of summer flowers
the shelter of leaves
the pecking of birds
and 'the darling buds of May'

choosing life and feeling is a fearful thing
makes one cry then sing
better indeed if fallow ground does break
then for calloused crust to guard the tender pulse
from the approaching storm....

life – our heart – our voice – our soul
the ground of our being
is exquisite
in its beauty and complexity

beware of building moats and fences
walls without doors
paths with closed gates
till no one even hears the shout

and tragically another unique voice
fades to a whisper
curled like an unborn child
within a womb of fear

to be born healthy and to grow well
is to never doubt the voice
that delights to cry and sing with an authentic ring
first limping free in awkward flight
then soaring on a wide-feathered wingspan
high above the crumbled human earth
where flowers bob heads in soft-tilled beds
colour-splashing row upon row upon row

Dead Man Writing –
Vancouver Airport (Jan. '97)

the last week has been hell

...a time-dungeon of blackness and voiceless gloom
where emotional voids and despair lurk like deep-sea bottom-
    feeders

except this ocean is mine that ebbs and flows beneath my
    surface skin
hiding the mysteries of my heart's underground
guilt has surfed across that ocean and through my mind
on waves of grief and longing
I can no longer tell where sin begins or good things end
where love is a gift or nurture a friend
or who is the enemy attacking me from within

tonight I'm at the airport – heading for Toronto
God only knows why
will He be there
it's a flight of despair

I feel like a man of 40-something on the outside
while inside a 4-year-old boy tries to hide
Rip van Winkle suddenly stirred now out of place
a little kid lost
no mother no father no welcoming face
no hand to take hold of
no one to embrace
every time I stop and think I choke

and tears well up out of the most broken heart
and tired spirit I have ever known

I look around with blank eyes
I'll do anything you want
my fight is gone – I have nothing left to give
just more aching and crying....
I squint over my shoulder and shake my head
for these voids released within
have dumped me like a drunk on a bench
an old bottle on a windswept beach
a deadbeat at a dead end
and now I don't know where to begin

that's me tonight – 4 going on 5
a broken pastor – a failed husband
a guilty father
a goldfish in a bowl

a dead man writing
crying in an airport for a friend
and for this excruciating pain inside
to end

A Man of Unclean Lips

"I am a man of unclean lips and I live among a people of unclean lips. ..." uttered the Prophet Isaiah nearly 3,000 years ago as he contemplated delivering a tough message to the people of Israel . He regarded himself as falling into the same category as those to whom he addressed his rhetoric. Isaiah confessed from the outset that the guilt and rebellion exposed and challenged by his words, was his guilt as well. I am no Isaiah, and I presume to bring no message from God. All that I can attempt to do is share my very ordinary story; to humbly articulate periods of my life where desolation and despair clung to my side like a barnacle is glued to a rock at high tide and will not be washed away.

Inevitably in the telling of such tales as these, personal ones of despair, lost hope and vision, it can appear as if all others are to blame for the predicament that was mine. The topic is painfully introspective, self-absorbing, and self-centred. In the telling of it blame and accusation is futile and such a focus is certainly not my motive, nor my intent. However, to attempt to find some reason why, and a better understanding of how these things happen, is, I believe, exceedingly worthwhile. Consequently, in the spirit of Isaiah, I too preface my utterances by confessing my culpability and my gross imperfection here, at this reflective beginning.

As I reference unfulfilled longings, rejection, and hurt, I am attempting to describe, articulate, and even validate the legitimacy and reality of such emotions – not to play the victim, the accuser, or the martyr. In every way that I have experienced misunderstanding and frustration from family, friends, and colleagues, I have regrettably contributed to similar feelings in others because of my ill-advised words, actions, and attitudes. Of course, for the most part

24

these actions and attitudes are not intentionally forged on the anvil of our beings with the purpose of doing damage – but they happen anyway – despite us. The fact is that we all live as people of unclean lips among others of similar affliction and unenviable disposition.

It is acceptable in our culture to break a leg, to be afflicted with cancer, or to endure an accident causing permanent injury. Invariably these unfortunate events evoke a response of compassion and caring from relatives and friends. In the hospital's intensive care unit visitors come and go, demanding nothing from the one who silently fights for life, other than dispensing encouraging words to 'get better' and 'listen to the doctors and nurses'.

However, when the pain is not physical, and the breakdown has no apparent physical symptom, responses are not always as gracious, nor quite as understanding. It is hard for the onlooker to comprehend 'what is going on' and therefore impatience, dismissal, quick fixes, or cynicism too frequently frame the unwittingly insensitive responses. We don't think for a moment of telling someone in the intensive care unit to snap out of their condition, yet when confronted with emotional struggles, we dispense advice and prescriptions with an expertise and an aplomb that invariably insults the integrity of the recipient.

The comment that infuriated me the most was 'you make your choices'; which somehow implied that with a deft flick of the intellectual switch all would fall neatly into place. I wish it were that simple. The ability to make good choices needs to be supported by encouragement, understanding, inner resolve and a myriad of other intangible elements. While I strongly advocate the importance of personal responsibility and living with the consequences of one's choices and actions, I also believe that sometimes we need to help each other arrive at a place where it is possible to 'decide and to choose wisely'.

In this collection of writings I am attempting to describe how depression and inner turmoil feels, smells, tastes, and appears; and how it was experienced by me. This is one mortal man's account riddled with subjective and relative reflections. The context is one of high Christian morality, teaching, belief, conviction, passion ... and personal struggle. I have not spent years in the workshop smoothing every rough edge or waiting for every feeling I had, and have, to subside into an attractive and acceptable form. There are some mellow and introspective places here as well as some raw and 'still-to-be-completed' areas that are far from healed and at rest.

A Fishing Boat

I saw it one night while strolling alone
beside the ebbing tide
its weathered form restlessly tethered
ten feet below toe level
a fishing boat moored at the harbor quay

a few days later
the boat rode high on the incoming tide
there was no need for looking down then

daylight's indifference
cruelly exposed her as tired and worn out
heavily worked dented torn
tangle-draped cables
aluminum under peeling paint
blistered wood roughed by calloused hands
rust marks sweating stains
through what once upon a time
were clean and neatly-pressed sides

that's me, I thought
chained to people church even marriage
up and down every day on the relentless surge of an
    emotional tide
worn out dented tear-stained and troubled

fishing nets were piled everywhere
but the ones that caught my eye lay bundled on the shore
cast aside in a broken frayed multi-coloured profusion of
    tangled knots

my spilled-out guts
I thought
bundles of broken despair
I wonder if I'll ever sail the seas again
right now I can't see it think it or feel it....

does anyone know how to repair
or untangle
me on the quay

Collapse

At first glance, no one would even have known that the Valley existed. From where I stood all I could see was barren landscape, sharp outcrops, clusters of boulders and rocks, and splintered shard fragments scattered over dusty ground. Vultures slowly circled high in a pale translucent sky. They traced a patient death spiral gliding effortlessly on the tips of invisible currents, mocking respect for the creatures frantically scurrying below to falter. I shivered at the sight, and prayed that they would never peck my flesh to the bone.

The bleak earthscape is one clue to the Valley's existence, as is the presence of 'the vultures' (self-appointed critics, from my perspective, who watch and undermine from a distance – guarding themselves while feeding on another's frailty). Hypersensitivity has the ability to transform turtledoves in flight into angry birds of prey when viewed from a distance.

Another 'sign' is the rumbling way below the earth's surface and the subsequent shifting from stability to instability beneath one's feet. There is a sense of a deep inner discontent, a void, a lost longing that, having awakened after a long sleep, draws all of one's being slowly and relentlessly into its vast emptiness. This is no ordinary terrain. It moves and changes like cold cracking glaciers that guard mountain peaks, and sometimes swallow luckless explorers who dare crampon crawl across their thick and fragile skin. There is a paradoxical beauty here, like the haunting wonder that wraps soft blankets of silence around the onlooker in the desert, the sunlit radiance of an Arctic plateau where the wind sighs and chills one to the marrow, or a beach where a riptide is camouflaged beneath innocent curling waves breaking rhythmically along the sand.

Likewise, melancholic introspection has its own mesmerizing quality. It can reveal fascinating insights and vistas of exquisite sensitivities that have lain buried and neglected for years. To excavate the ruins and wreckage of emotional breakdown is undoubtedly anthropologically and psychologically fascinating – until one becomes the subject, that is.

The transition from barren plateau into the Valley is inevitably different for each person. However I suspect that the common thread woven through the tapestry of all our realities is some intensification of pressure that becomes the 'last straw'.

Each contributing factor on its own (whether personal or job-related) would have been manageable for me. However, as they relentlessly flowed and fused together they produced an emotional melting pot that began to absorb me into itself – and I sank into the quicksand of a floundering identity. I seemed to have spent so much of my time trying to seek God's will and to 'be there' for others that 'I' struggled to know where 'I' was, or what had become of 'me'. While others had unravelled in the privacy of my office during countless hours of 'counselling', I felt I was disintegrating in a goldfish bowl from which there was no escape; and nobody understood my dilemma.

For those who have been fortunate enough to avoid these dark places I plead for patience and understanding. My descriptions and recollections will appear very self-absorbed and nauseatingly self-centred; it will appear as if I am suggesting that everyone else was to blame for my predicament. For a while that is precisely what it feels like. Objective truth and reality hold no power in the struggle to make sense of what happens. The only priority is to survive the brutal honesty and vulnerability of what feels like a broken heart and a crushed spirit, tossed like garbage on a dump of gut-wrenching despair.

Inevitably the 'one step too many or last straw' reveals the entrance to the Valley as a sinkhole of darkness, depths, and voids. With alarming swiftness and a vice-like embrace it tugs victims down into its darkness and hidden places. It is like a crocodile springing, pouncing, snapping, and pulling its prey from the land to be buried in a watery grave. The place of entry is a crashing fall over a cliff of despair. Sometimes this is anticipated but I suspect the intensity is a surprise to most. Tired tentative footsteps finally slip and weary legs no longer support the burdened body and soul they have graciously carried for so long. The facades and outer protection peels and melts away and all the grotesque and disfiguring pain encapsulates you in a hideous garment of shame and sorrow. All is revealed and laid bare, and everyone around you now sees and knows (or thinks they do); the humiliation is complete.

Loneliness

I used to be an expert

you could come and visit me at any time
I would listen and dispense advice
talk of principles and things to do
and sincerely try to be there for you

a few said I was even quite good at 'counselling'

I used to struggle to understand why some people wrestled so
much
they just didn't try
didn't want to deal with their issues
I said I would pray
and ask God to help them
Jesus to love them
and the Holy Spirit to fill them

I sincerely tried to be there for them
it made me feel good to be needed and wise to advise
if 'they' only would listen
then one day they too could be strong and stable – like me

but now I'm faced with truth that x-rays through my being
exposing just how little I actually understood
the experts irritate me
and sometimes I think of counselors as human mechanics
and I'm not sure anymore what 'helping' really means

as I dispensed my counsel
I became increasingly aware of other knockings at my door
which for a time I preferred to ignore
until one day they had the audacity to goosestep inside
quite unannounced and uninvited

press-ganging me to the floor
loneliness depression and despair introduced themselves
as I cowered beneath my counsellor's chair
no one else was there

I never knew how strong they could be
crushing oppression at every bend
along a road of unending turmoil
who cares about theories now I cried
as earth-quaking heartaches shock-waved and tremored
flooding my mind and drowning thoughts
with wave after wave
of feelings

rolling and breaking rolling and breaking rolling and breaking
rolling and breaking rolling and breaking rolling and breaking
rolling and breaking rolling and breaking rolling and breaking

along my logically principled shoreline
shipwrecking my confidence
reducing the rational to a chaotic rubble

loneliness surprised me the most with his power to overwhelm
he'd suddenly show his face in a crowded room or a solitary
        place
never alone
always accompanied by depression or despair
sleazy henchmen clad in trench coats
collars upturned against the cold night air

condemnation was often there as well
even suicide gamely shuffled alongside

33

lifting a cloak-flap to furtively reveal what he had to offer
at first glance it was quite an impressive array
but on closer inspection they were cheap gaudy trinkets
how I dreaded those awful encounters
I wouldn't call it company

Gray Heron

a few days before Christmas
the gray heron stood frozen
like a statue on a rock in winter

the lamp light was bright
snow fell cold
gentle white and softly
touching down on ground and tree
feather-light
breathtaking
quite still and quiet

in the lap of the shore at the lip of the tide
the bird watched me wander
beady black eyes tracing my pacing
going nowhere real slow

a gray heron on a gray rock on a gray night
with nowhere to fly
snow mantled his back
and capped his head
like a wise old rabbinic professor

but the aged-looking bird never shook them off
he didn't seem to care....
we're a fine pair, I said,
alone out here with snow on our head
he turned away

that's what loneliness does much of the time
turns me away from what others say
chokes my throat with thick lumps
and fills me with gray
passion drains
and words empty of form
silence fills the vacuum and I walk alone

This is no Eden

I read today that the Lord is close to the brokenhearted
and to those whose spirits are crushed
that must be me

I don't feel His presence too close right now

this emotional landscape is not a pleasant place
certainly no Eden where joy and hope grow lush
and love rushes quick down biblical hillsides of delight
where milk and honey flow thick and sweet
and life is to know the presence of the Lord

no, this landscape is lunar stark
etched black
dust-rock dark
devoid of life
God's backyard

it's a place where discarded bits and pieces randomly clutter
    the ground
throwbacks from when the Creator carefully whittled His
    perfect world
it's where beauty is viewed as far away in another place
inaccessible and unattainable from this vantage point
where I watch and exist in seeming isolation

kind people come to visit and talk
but in this depression of mind
it's hard to find the motivation to walk another mile

or to muster the strength to conjure up
even one more appreciative smile

it's a slow lonely and cruel orbit through space
and for those who travel at this excruciating pace
there's no beginning or end
no mercy – no grace
caught in the tug of mind heart and will
straining at the innermost core
spirit crushed and heart broken
desperately waiting for God's presence to break through

and that's about all you can do
from this bleak
bleak point of view

Cracks Appear

The metamorphosis in the landscape of my psyche was so gradual I scarcely noticed any change at all.

As the chill in the air and the turning of the leaves gently introduces the fall, so the increased frequency of 'gray days' evoked an occasional shiver within my being. Naïvely I ignored them and brushed them aside as the pressure or tiredness that would pass with 'an early night'. Fleeting visitations of depression, wisps of futility, moments of disillusionment, days without joy and nights of musing – one by one they slipped through the veil and quietly took up residence. Life went on much the same for quite a long while; but the beginnings and ends and borders – where one thing leads to another, I could neither discern nor comprehend.

Inevitably a day finally dawned when I awoke to find the surrounding terrain as bleak as a wind-swept dune on a winter's day. The first hint of change began when the sparkling array of flowers, and my enthusiastic interaction with people shrivelled and curled into a mundane apathy. Indifferent cataracts formed and melted all things visible into a mediocre sameness before my wandering and disinterested eyes. It was as if colour-blindness had crept in and quietly drawn the curtains over the sun, closing the shutters over my eyes and spirit, and subduing the room of my world into a dull twilight zone.

Because the transformation evolved so gradually I didn't really recognize the dimming of the light; apart from periodically squinting and subconsciously registering that 'something was amiss'. Things that used to cause me to be passionate and engaged left me cold and indifferent. Stamina and enthusiasm trickled away through the cracks of a faltering self-esteem and a growing sense of disillusionment. At the same time my hearing also seemed to concertina in and out. In Stephen Spielberg's movie *Saving Private Ryan*, there are moments where in the midst of trauma and the bloody action of warfare all sound ceases. The effect is eerie. One sees the action, knows guns are blazing and people are shouting, but without the noise being registered the effect is as if the person involved is one dimension removed from the action. The participant becomes an onlooker even while still embroiled in the action. To others around – nothing has changed – but to the one without hearing a radical transformation has taken place that is invisible to the naked eye. The silence forms a surreal bubble around the individual, separating them from … while maintaining the appearance of still being in the midst of.…

Another 'visual trick' that makes this place so hard to fathom for the onlooker, and so depressingly difficult to communicate for the 'traveller', is the totally different perspective each has of the present reality. For the 'traveller', the surroundings are as I have described – bleak and barren. There is no 'New Jerusalem' to look forward to, giving hope and the promise of a future victory, triumph, and glory. The future has no city on the horizon, just shimmering mirages and tremoring waves of nothingness.

As far as I was concerned the 'New Jerusalem' lay behind me, a pile of rubble and smoking ruins, broken promises and tumbledown dreams. All that I had hoped for, or aspired to, crashed around me. Not in a sudden explosion caused by one catastrophic event, but rather in a long slow-motion collapse – imploding from the inside out. And the mushroom cloud of depression that accompanied that long event brought with it suffocating despair, anger, and a gnawing sense of futility concerning everyone and everything that had once held meaning.

I had walked with eyes downcast for a long time, concentrating on placing one foot before the other. The journey had become the focus, survival the goal. Doing my job and praying to God for the tensions to ease was my preoccupation. But the barrenness of the land and the blurring of vision only served to highlight my own inner thirst. Then I felt the tremors.

Up and Down

every now and then when I stretch and
balance on tip-toe at the shaky rim of my emotions
I sometimes see beyond the self-absorbed horizons
of bleak despair
and catch a glimpse
of the first faint rays of better days

but my desperate pirouette is hard to sustain
and almost inevitably I fall backwards
downwards
and
inwards
tumbling
free-falling
into the crack
yawning and tearing wider the mind and heart
splitting ever deeper
ripping
prizing apart
somersaulting confusions
inside out revolutions
within
what I used to call – me
but the final crash never comes
and the fall never ends

my life suspends on countless pendulum swings
from the rim of hope
into a hell-hole of despair
bungee-bouncing back for a promise fulfilled

then disillusioned gravitating down
crying damn shame
I'll never hope or believe again

Honesty

to be perfectly honest
do you really want to know what I feel and long for
my joys and my sorrows

should I say what I think
should I write it down and
articulate the hope and fear
about why I despair

these times are so hard for those close by
the truth is too painful
it's kinder and easier to lie
what is the truth

to be perfectly honest
this endless refrain of love lost and pain
will drive us insane
some feel rejected by what's said and done
and others are defeated
by what can never be won
for some there is hope
filled with the anticipation of change
while others have no more rope
and are left destitute
as their thread's run out bare

to be perfectly honest
it's difficult to know which way is best
or which way forward to go....

Wilderness

where are You, God
in this bleak wilderness of spirit and soul

is this simply all my own doing
the unfolding desert of wind-feathered dunes
shifting sands blowing encroaching chaos
suffocatingly brash and bold
in a most intimate of lands

I know I'm not whole but then who is
I've confessed the darkness within
and the places I've been
I'm numbed by Your absence and afraid of Your presence
I resentfully question every commitment

how did I get here
to the edge of this despair
a lone wolf wailing
exhausted and struggling
orphaned
restlessly wandering
angry and hurting like hell

my ranting and raving
sounds like such a pathetic plea to me
I am embarrassed to give voice to my immaturity
and yet it begs from within for validation

I've given all I can give
and have struggled to live in a manner pleasing to You

honouring Your Word and Your Name
I've spoken and taught and stood up for 'truth'
but Jesus right now it feels like for naught
I'm bruised by Your body
and the countless demands
the subtle inflections
the polite reprimands
the layers of rejection
and the turning of friends
the in-fighting out-falling have taken their toll
and this wounded soldier
is bleeding and broken
and so goddamned tired of it all

self-pity rises dank and damp
like a mist over trenches at dawn
where bloody ego's are corpses
and mangled nerves contort
writhing and tortured
death kneels gravely at the feet of the wounded
hope is aborted
as the 'Last Post' wails from a trumpeter's horn

I lie low
barely breathing
where are You
who are You
God

I'm a coin lost in a crack
a sheep wandering astray
a son crying to get back to his Father some day
rejection has pierced
disillusioned I stand
foolish and naked reaching out for a....

God, I don't know anything anymore

Feelings

it's strange being numb day after day
with frostbitten feelings frozen in time
afraid that if thawed they'll hurt even more

feelings – once friends upon whom I'd depend
now shout and fight and are hard to trust
they tease – taunt
mock and haunt with a relentless pressure
and a demonic pleasure that scares me – to death

it used to be I who would give directions
call commands and control reactions
my mind was my own
independent
powerfully alone
now that's no longer true
I've been turned upside down by an emotional coup

or are these feelings really revealing old truths
that only good friends would dare mention
can I blame them for exposing my innermost core
or should I thank them
embrace them
and listen for more

The Loneliest Place on Earth

yesterday
I finished re-reading a book about Tristan da Cunha
an island in the South Atlantic

I remember childhood memories of refugees escaping to Cape
    Town by boat
fleeing a volcanic explosion that threatened to destroy their
    remote island home

Tristan da Cunha was a place battered by winds
and as far away as one could imagine being from 'civilization'

the author of the book
I went to school with his son
calls it the loneliest place on earth
where people live in thatched stone houses
consume home-grown potatoes and eat fish
caught from little boats fashioned by local hands
out of canvas and wood

I wonder if he's right about Tristan da Cunha being the
    loneliest place on earth
or are there places yet to travel where company is hard to find
regions not tucked away in some distant geographical crack
but closer than beyond the distant curve where land meets sky
and horizons halt the gaze of a wistfully searching eye

not long ago I stumbled upon my 'lonely place'
as I trod a track all overgrown
that led way back to my inner land

throughout my life faint echoes scents and sounds
hinted of its presence
but I never guessed from whence they came
nor what they meant
until sorrow acting as my guide beckoned silently
to that shoreline where my very essence
had found shape and form

initially I came to sight-see
and perhaps explore
but now the novelty has long past
and I can no longer casually withdraw

this island feels very isolated and very far away
no longer an interesting holiday touring the intricacies within
like some ancient honeycomb cave with stalagmites and
stalactites
instead I've lost my way amidst the twists and turns of this
subterranean maze
and my distorted vision has degenerated into a foggy haze

Tristan da Cunha looks like New York from here
I'm scared that I might have stumbled upon my loneliest place
on earth
an Alcatraz of sorts from which there is no escape
no easy out
no waking from a dream

even my volcanic screams falter and shrink into infant
whispers
against the raging tide of condemnation that rips my pride
and mocks with wet embrace my vain attempts to escape this
ravaged place
the shores of my inner being sink into an ocean of bleak
meaninglessness
that surrounds and stretches through ragged heaving waves
as far as my eye can see

I pace these sands day by day praying for some soul to appear
someone to ease my isolation
but alas no Good Friday walks this beach to impress his foot
    upon the sand
nor leave an imprint of hope for this dejected Crusoe to find

a naked Cross stands high on the hill
like a flag post once planted by explorers staking a claim for
    their king

that's me too

but even He whom I have long-called friend
eludes me in this bitter end
as blindly I struggle in desperately tired despair
grasping straws and clutching air
once again I feel ignored
finding nothing
touching no one
in panicked frustration
it's empty out there and so lonely in here
my mind beckons backward
saying He and they are not far away
but right here my heart seethes
abused and betrayed
I want to rip out my past and start over again
to hell with what's right I'll smash out the Light

despite myself I cannot take flight
for here in the midst of my stormy emotions and rebellious
    solutions
His whisper persists even as I resist
with hands over ears recounting my fears
sobbing I fall screaming my pain
awaiting rebuke and more judgement again
but nothing is given
no harsh word is said

everything's spoken in the silence instead
He lifts my face gently till my eyes rest on Him
He tells me that He knows all that I am
He shows me His tears mixed with the Blood of the Lamb
and the compassion and the mercy
and the strong broken hands
reaching out
reaching down
reaching into this man
then He turns me to look at the Cross on the hill
and the pain it demanded to lay down self-will
my rebellion is spent
"help me," I cry "to know how to die
I'm afraid of the pain that passion will bring
of hoping and trying and failing again and again"

standing on the shoreline of my innermost being
where meaning is found in the deepest of grieving
I pray for more faith
for help in believing that this dead man will rise again in the
    morning
and will walk restored in the land of the living

Gethesemane

this mid-life Gethsemane is certainly not
a fragrant garden scented with roses
indeed the long jealous stems of perfumed flowers so
    treasured by lovers
when woven locked and intertwined become a bloody crown
    of thorns
that's all too real in this hallowed place
above me is the furrowed face of One
whose will was yielded here to that of Another
for those such as I who later would appear

lost sheep wandering with bleating cry
seeking entrance to a Kingdom
whose way is narrow and whose gate is small
where to enter in is to relinquish all

today I crawl on bended knee to this Cross-roads
    this Gethsemane
where olive trees slowly rise and twist
from God's most ancient earth
miraculously their gnarled and deformed branches
still give birth to fruit that light the lamps
as pounding feet do crush and stamp
the cracking and the broken skin
until from their tender flesh within
pure oil flows

beneath the maturing boughs of these same trees
the lessons learned are hard to hear and cruel to see
not easily discerned

for in the breaking and pressing of olive and grape
pours life divine in oil and wine
"not my will but Thine" echoes down the ages
as disciples and pilgrims fill history's pages
with selfless choices of courageous martyrdom

now too for me this Gethsemane must be
no garden bed in which to sleep
but a place of anguish and travail
as I my watch do keep
with Peter I would agree
and rather flee to cast my nets again
in some distant tranquil Galilee
but even there I'd see the look
and feel the sting of guilt's sharp hook
as I denied what's true and turned

let this cup pass is my heart's cry
I have not will to live
nor strength to die
empty of resolve and filled with fear
I ask You Lord
to help me stand
lift this pilgrim
this prodigal
this wayward son
with Your stronger hand
let Your heart be mine
and Your love beat strong
that it may not be long
before I sing Your song
once more

Merry-go-round

this emotion and pulsating heartache beats relentlessly
as mind-numbing thoughts inch through time at a snail's pace
with psychopathic precision and little haste
laying waste to family and friends who
bravely try and stay this tortuous course with me

selfishly I limp along giving little cheer
unable to be strong for those who are near
like some drunk somnambulist
I rummage through my cluttered drawers
what's mine is mine what's yours is yours
I callously shout
as I stagger and stumble across tidy floors
breaking hearts and opening sores
talking with incoherent mumbles
about not caring anymore

the journey is long and the signposts few
too many wrong turnings
bill-boarded captions offer relief for pain
shouting and waving seductive refrains
suggesting advising with a mocking disdain
a miracle cure
a crutch for the lame

I'm told to communicate my feelings
and to reveal my heart
to grieve my losses and longings
and to pick all things apart

but others are here who breathe and bleed
and they're cut to the core by what I say is true

as I write and speak seeking meaning and purpose
hope and helpless
tussle like belligerent twins
how are you I'm questioned
don't ask
I reply
it's up and it's down
and I can't tell you why
on this merry-go-round
I get dizzy just sitting
the world is blurred
guts stir and churn
eyes flood
heart races
spinning and spurned
tomorrow's too far in the future
to make any plans....
but you don't understand....
do you

quite out of the blue
the next day is calm
a tranquil lagoon
peace relieves despair
the vistas are clear
and while hope's entertained
acceptance shyly draws near

panic and patience offer assistance
but declining their presence
I withdraw into numbness

this merry-go-round
spins silently

circling around and around
the same old ground

but those who should know
because they've been here before
tell me not to be impatient
take one day at a time
every struggle and emotion's
one less revolution
toward an end to this hell

Battlefield

like a ragamuffin doll
flicked and jerked
on a wild dog's snout
fangs catch and release tearing me
ripping inside until the stuffing's raked out
and there's no more challenge
no more fight

the battle moves on
distracted and bored
the demon dog leaves
but the warfare still rages
I'm caught in the crossfire
a sitting duck etched on the skyline

right now I'm afraid
and really don't care
shell-shocked and bleeding
I haven't a clue what hit me
when gripped with despair
something snapped inside
catapulting me slow motion through the air

in a month of Sundays
I never dreamed I'd ever be in need of such repair
so wounded on the inside
so vulnerable and weak
so destitute of faith and pride
so utterly unable to even want to speak
the ones who really helped

enlisted few words and threw no stones
instead they offered love
saturated in grace and gifts
filled with space and acceptance
they let me be

but that damn dog's not gone for good
indeed it's for evil that he hunts and prowls
and even as I slowly heal
I feel his breath and hear his growls
in the darkest hours
when he paws outside my door
sniffing and scratching
wanting and craving
more and more and more
of me

all I can do is trust that others will
defend my life this night
I cry out to God
to cleanse and heal
the roots and reasons
for the deep things I feel
and that there will come a time
when I will be restored
and the water once more
will taste like wine

but from where I lie in this ragged heap right now
that dream is vague and very far away

Can't Breathe!

I used to suffer with asthma as a child. The doctor said it was because of nervousness and that I would grow out of it. I worried a lot about going to school, about what would happen to me, about family and friends. Insecurity felt familiar and there were very few knees to bounce on or grown-ups to snuggle into and hear reassurances from. My worries remained bottled up for a time and then would exorcize themselves through eczema and my heaving lungs gasping for breath.

The first remedy I remember was a hot bowl of water mixed with Friar's Balsam at my grandmother's home, where we lived for a while. A towel was draped over my wheezing head as I was encouraged to breathe in the steaming vapours for relief. I was taken to the hospital for x-rays and stood in a black box with a few little red lights and I cried because I was afraid and alone in a dark and strange place.

Nervous apprehension was very much a part of my disposition in my formative years. I was afraid of doing things wrong and getting into trouble, afraid of visiting with friends and staying overnight, afraid that my parents wouldn't come home at night. I would often lie awake imagining a car crash and breathe a quiet sigh of relief when I heard the car decelerate or the key turn in the lock. I rocked myself to sleep for years forming a cradle with one hand behind my head and the other under my back – then I would sway from side to side and quietly sing – and think … until I went to sleep. I also sucked my thumb in private until I was about ten.

One night the asthma struck with a vengeance and I walked up and down the hallway frantically clawing for air. There was no relief and

I thought I would die. Maybe my parents did too. They called the doctor, who was a kind and gentle man. He arrived to the desperate phone call in the middle of the night and gave me an injection and a pill to swallow. I promptly vomited all over the place and then must have settled down. I did grow out of those terrible attacks but will never forget their throttling grip around my throat.

Self-nurture began at an early age. Of course my parents were around but I don't recall us talking to one another or developing any sense of intimacy. In the early years I would comb dad's hair and play at being his barber. He told us stories about Captain Hook that scared and thrilled my brother and me before we went to sleep dreaming of pirate ships.

My Father

you want me to talk about my father

I have mixed feelings about attempting to do that
I'd rather chat of other matters
which in itself should tell you
all you really need to know

we were not close
I called him dad
he called me son but
we never had a friendship
to fill those unique and private places
only a father's grace nurtures in his child

my father devoured books
and he read deeply and widely
he loved to walk in the mountains
lie in the sun
swim far out to sea and bodysurf
walk salt-water dripping up the beach
running his fingers through his gray wiry hair
he was exhilarated and content by any ocean

dad played sport with passion
deriving great joy in competing
it didn't matter who won
as long as everyone played fair and had fun
he was an honest fair-minded man
not one for adventure or chance
he liked routine and order

a hand of bridge
two fingers of gin
a glass of wine
evenings to dance and dine
with friends who went back a long way
and when Brian finally exited the stage
they had kind things to say
memories and tears
jokes and stories aplenty
as usual I wasn't there
half by choice and half by circumstance
instead
I listened to the eulogy on a tape recording
and despised my envy

my father was a good man
I believe he tried his best
with all that he'd been given
but to me he was more of a stranger than a dad
a figure viewed from afar

dad struggled to reach out and draw me to his side
it didn't help that I reacted and pulled further wide
he never told me he loved me
nor that he took pride in the things I had done
or that one of his great delights
was my being his son
though I journeyed over half a world as his end drew near
he still maintained his distance
as I struggled with mine

we talked about nothing over mugs of beer
and at our final departing no visible tear was spilled
just a shaking of hands and a formal good-bye
my inside said hug him
but my outside declined
like father like son we remained

stubborn and proud of mind
now I look back in anger
the void penetrates deep
a family of strangers is what we became
with little in common except for a name

the blessing when given becomes a curse when denied
love fulfilled will never be found
floating in a spiritual realm
in sporadic passionate liaisons
or even intellectual abstractions
it's all that and more

love needs skin and bone
and when a father withholds it
for no matter the reason
his children are betrayed
by an act of great treason
in his hand and his heart alone
lie the essence of love
the priceless ingredient
self-esteem's seed
which if neglected or not nurtured
allows the curse to travel on down
like when dad's father's hand
never took hold of his son

The Beach

My father would take us to the beach most summer weekends and we sang songs in the car that included.… "One man went to mow, went to mow a meadow, one man and his dog went to mow a meadow.…" or "Ten green bottles sitting on a wall, what if one bottle should accidentally fall, there'd be nine green bottles.…"

We often went to Dalebrook; it had a tidal seawater-pool to play in and lots of rocks and pools to explore. I managed to 'doggy-paddle' in that pool for the first time and stay afloat without my feet touching the ground. I could swim! I loved those times. A few years later the great thrill would be to stand on the pool wall when the tide was high and try not to get washed off balance by the surging waves as they broke over us. The one who remained standing the longest was King of the Wall for a reign of epic brevity!

While we amused ourselves dad read his book and then swam out into the deep sea beyond the protected confines of the pool; he was a very good swimmer and throughout his life enjoyed an abiding love affair with the ocean. As I grew older I would delight in threading bait onto a hook and trying to catch the little fish that darted around the rock pools. They were slippery, slimy, ugly, and tiny – but oh what joy when one was landed and wriggled at our feet! Then came the worst part – trying to retrieve the hook from a gaping mouth without appearing to be nervous or slightly scared.

On other occasions, depending on the strength and direction of the wind, we embarked on a twenty-minute drive from home to Sunrise beach where the real waves rolled in. This was just one portion of miles and miles of white sandy beaches that form a bleached surf-ruffled collar around False Bay. After a swim and bodysurfing we would walk along the hard sand below the high tide line and collect shells, and maybe be lucky enough to find some fishermen hauling in their nets.

The fishermen evoked the greatest excitement and activity on the beach. They heaved their wooden boats out over the waves straining against the oars as they crested and ploughed through the breaking surf. One person in the stern unraveled a long net as the boat carved a crescent-moon offshore before surfing back onto the beach. Then began the arduous task of hauling in the nets. The whole activity always attracted a crowd of onlookers complete with a host of hungry squawking seagulls cawing and swooping for a free meal.

Everyone on the beach grabbed a portion of the net or rope to help pull in the catch amidst much shouting, laughter and excitement. After what seemed like an eternity the first fish appeared, and then more and more flopped up the beach bounced by the dripping net. Crabs scurried out, seaweed was untangled, the odd shark or stingray was displayed, and then the gleaming silver fish were counted and auctioned off right there at the high tide line.

Driving home from the beach it was not unusual to see fish being sold at the side of the road by enthusiastic men offering a great price for their 'fresh fish'. Back in the suburbs I still remember the plaintiff sound of the fisherman blowing his horn; it was made from dried seaweed and he constantly wailed through it as he coaxed his horse and cart through the streets offering his produce for sale.

Scottish Ferry

I remember riding the ferry from Iona to Oban
off the wild disheveled western shore
of Scotland's heathered form
darkness ambushed our homeward run
and the sea ran amuck a-heaving and a-bucking
above the sound of our chattering teeth
we could hear the wind whistle and roar
in a haunting highland yodel

accompanying the wind's frenzied refrain
the sea-spray intercepted the rain
and they energetically danced with a hell-bent abandon
in their uninhibitedly wet domain

I watched from the stern sheltered by the cabin
as the old boat ploughed through the elements
with a confident strength and an assurance I envied
it broad-shouldered the onslaught of wind rain and sea
safely protecting passengers such as me
like an old fisherman in rain gear would
cradle a child in the crook of his arm

and in that place where I stood
behind the stack and the captain's back
there was great peace and a calm in the eye of the storm
I felt surprisingly sheltered and safe
on the ferry's salt-weathered deck

the seagulls know how to fly when the weather is rough
they tuck into the slipstream and glide easily home

I watched their effortless rising and falling with wonder
as they calmly out-maneuvered this hell
by hardly moving a wing
better pay attention and learn this lesson well

Walks With My Father

Every winter my father would embark on Sunday afternoon walks in the mountains. One day it would be through Kirstenbosch Botanical Gardens and then up the boulder-strewn path of Skeleton Gorge on the slopes of Devil's Peak. Another day we would drive past the Rondebosch Zoo, where the lions roared, and through the Cape pine trees that bent like tall gray giraffes over our heads to Rhodes Memorial. Situated higher up the mountain slopes behind the University of Cape Town this granite memorial resembles a Greek temple; it commemorates the vision of Cecil John Rhodes to build a road from Cape Town to Cairo. The great symmetrical granite steps are lined with larger-than-life lions cast in bronze, weathered black-green and shining in places where many hands and knees have pressed and rubbed. They gaze over the Peninsula with wise and patient stares and they never growl when little boys ride their backs, stroke their thick manes and whisper secrets into their ears.

We would walk along the Contour Path or scramble up to the old fort from where one can survey the Cape Flats. In clear weather it is possible to glimpse the shorelines of both the Atlantic and Indian oceans on either side of the Peninsula. On one occasion my father and I hiked up the mountain from Constantia Nek and walked across the flat summit, where there was a large reservoir. For some obscure reason which I can no longer recall I started walking down the mountain backwards; and for a mere five-cent bet from dad I proceeded to continue this strange behaviour all the way to the bottom. Needless to say there were some curious glances from the few hikers whom we met on our way down.

Another trip I enjoyed was scrambling up Lion's Head. The attraction was found near the summit, where the chains bolted to the rock face assisted our final ascent to the white graffiti-scarred beacon marking the peak. From that vantage point the whole of Cape Town spread out below our feet; Table Bay, the Twelve Apostles, Robben Island, and the distant shore of Bloubergstrand tucked in the curve of the coastline.

These were probably some of the happiest times I enjoyed with my father. It looked like a foundation upon which we could forge a friendship – but for all the myriad of reasons imaginable we never managed to build more or climb higher. What might have been still lingers....

Offering Up Isaac

did I hear you right Lord
my son
a sacrifice

the promised one
of whom your angels told
would fill barren Sarah's womb
when she was old
far beyond the normal years of motherhood

You promised
that the one given life from my dead loins
would from her explode
to be the first of many
as numerous as the stars
you flung so lavishly across a dark desert sky
to light the night and guide
countless generations of passersby

You said so

remember that night
when you showed me your exquisite creativity
suspended under heaven's vast canopy
and they were to be my children
Abraham's descendants

You promised

and now this call
this cruel command
that makes no sense at all
with no logical form or reason
at least to me
give up Isaac

he through whom so much was promised
he upon whom we looked and loved
with marvelling eyes
unfathomable delight
and devoted pride
he who brought us such unexpected joy and life
in our latter years
now to be slaughtered
butchered
by his own father's hand
sliced under my sharpened blade
how can this be

except
that I have learned that You are God
and I am mere man
his birth I did not understand
why should I now begin to comprehend
the meaning of his end

Isaac's trust was so complete

with slow and ponderous feet
we climbed Moriah's bloody rock
a threshing floor of the Lord
whom once I had thought
I knew

all I have loved lies here bound
and I scarce can stand

an agonizing father pleading with his God
from a heart whose every beat brings pain
words have ceased
to adequately convey
what this tattered love would say
and the wide-eyed child
what of him
whose life is given and taken
at his Creator's whim
while a helpless father sheds
tears like rain over the little one to whom
he cannot explain within the realm of love
or common sense
the meaning of this obedience
demanded of him

slowly and tenderly
he prepares the gruesome living sacrifice
until with no way out
his shaking hand rises
poised to stab and kill

but what's that
a noise close by arrests the final plunge
a bleating cry
reveals Another's will whose love
stills the agonized hand
shaking above the child's head
and accepts a ram to die instead

Isaac is free to live

silently they complete the glorious and bloody deed
then rise and leave behind
one life given one life denied
charred blood and bones
on a pile of smoldering stones

could I do that I wonder
give back when asked
and somehow offer up my Isaacs to You
I want reasons and answers to my cry
before I tread that dead-end walk
up Mount Moriah's side to die

is this a bluff you toss my way
to test how tough is my resolve
to live the things I say

the heart hears
yearns
and seeks to express
what the mind
has not yet begun to sense
or think right though

thus the tense straining between the two
leading us here to this Moriah
where we struggle
me and You

Morning Star

at first glimpse
could this possibly be
the morning star that blinks
then quietly withdraws
making way for dawn
the handmaid of the one majestic
brilliant sun

thus begins the daily etch and wash
of colours draped and veiled
transforming the sky from almost black
through inky blue to a brighter hue
and then other shades hidden yet unseen
till darkness finally fades
and light reveals to waiting earth
another morning's birth

I'm scared to hope
maybe I dream
for it has been so long a night alone
where despair has been my chaperone

perhaps it's true
that time and prayer helps hope break through
as sunshine burns away the misty fog
carelessly discarded across the threshold
of every naïve new day

I know that all is not complete
for the wounds are tender

and when I move and interact with others
I still feel the pain and loneliness
of wondering who really understands
all that has transpired

even as healing slowly halts the bleeding
scars form on heart and tattered skin
tattoos roughly drawn
yet forever worn
telling a tale and recording for years
these long and lonely times of grief and loss
of strife
and of many many tears

One Question?

If I were only allowed to ask you one question in order to learn something about who you are, it would be, "What kind of relationship did you have with your father?"

I would be interested to know as much as you were willing to tell me about that relationship. Your answer would provide us with major insights into better understanding issues of self-worth and self-esteem, confidence, identity, sexuality, perception of God, and attitude toward authority. This is not the place to enter into a long dissertation; I merely offer the suggestion that has emerged from many years of asking that question to others, as well as pondering it myself. The answer has nothing to do with blame, and everything to do with gaining at least a partial insight into explaining how and why we develop and grow into adulthood as we do.

While the mother-child relationship is naturally and intuitively deep and strong and foundational, it is the father-child relationship that significantly impacts the development and identity of men and women into adulthood. I have long reflected on the words that God the Father spoke to His Son Jesus at His baptism in the Jordan River before He began His grueling public ministry. They were words from the heart of a Father intended to nurture the heart of His Son, and they were stated publicly for everyone to hear. Of all the things He could have said, the fact that these were the words He chose for such an important occasion is worth noting.

"This is my Son, Whom I love, and in Whom I am well pleased."

Why are these words significant? I think it is because they underscore a profound truth about who we are and about our core needs and makeup. It is no accident that in the Christian faith God is revealed as 'Father'. Unfortunately in our somewhat self-centred and intellectually arrogant and egotistical western culture some have seen fit to attempt to rewrite the Biblical account in order to render God as meaning anything but 'Father'. They would rather talk about mother, great power, unseen spirit, or whatever other names you can think of. In my naïveté such 'revisionism' communicates more about our hang-ups and wounds than I think it says about God's identity. If I introduce myself to you as John and you keep calling me Pat – your choice of words does not change the reality of my name or identity, in fact I would regard you as being rude.

The problem is that all of our experiences on this earth concerning 'fathers' are somewhat distorted and 'less than perfect'. Maybe parents on this earth are really custodians and surrogate parents who have been entrusted with the gift of children for a while. Their task is to nurture them, love them, and provide for them in a manner that enables them to have a strong sense of identity, purpose, and meaning in the world. But at the end of the day every surrogate parent is limited, which is why another responsibility they have is to introduce their children to their real parent and Creator, God the Father – which is how He has introduced Himself. The words He spoke over Jesus are the same words He speaks over every human being to whom He has given the gift of life. The question is whether we ever hear and receive the depth of the love those words intend to convey. The temptation I have now is to want to qualify my statements and to provide a rationale for every 'but' that might spring to mind as you read these thoughts. Unfortunately this is not the time or place; however, the conversation is important.

"This is my Son, Whom I love, and in Whom I am well pleased."

These words were spoken in public for others to hear as well. When a father boasts about his child in public he blesses his child and helps foster a pride and a self-esteem that is so essential for a well-grounded sense of identity.

"This is my Son (or Daughter)." – Every human being needs to know to whom they belong. Which is why every adopted person naturally and instinctively yearns to know who their real blood-parents are, while at the same time being terrified that in searching they might discover that they really were not wanted after all. The identity of being someone's son or daughter provides a context with meaning, culture, roots, and a background – all of which provides a sense of history and belonging.

"Whom I love." – It's more than words describing a relationship, isn't it? The power is in the love conveyed that affirms a sense of belonging, of being deeply valued, precious, and cared for. They are words confirming that a person is important to someone (particularly a parent), and if Jesus needed to hear and know such a truth, then I guess we all do.

"In Whom I am well pleased." – God the Father goes even further in His lavish affirmation to underline the fact that Jesus pleases Him. Children of any age need to frequently hear from their parents that they are a delight and pleasure to them; such words provide a healing balm of inestimable value.

Remove these simple words and the experience of a core relationship with their father from a person's life and we should not be surprised that emotional confusion, insecurity, and a lifelong struggle with self-identity inevitably follows. I know that connecting with God the Father made a huge impact on the direction of my life and helped fill some of the voids. However, the depression exposed the hidden areas that still needed healing at more than just an intellectual level. While that caused me great anger and disillusionment, I still believe it is part of the process of planting the truth of those words more deeply in my soul. At the same time, understanding why it has to be so hard remains a mystery.

An Echo

there's something quite strange
about the space I'm in
a place of bitter sweetness
of fragile emptiness
honeycombed with many chambers
where the aroma of the nectar lingers
but the substance
once suspended gold
has long gone

I feel like an echo
disembodied
resounding
bouncing between rocky canyon walls
floating free from the one who
gave birth to the sound
unsure of where my end will be
or how I'll hit the ground

once I nearly drowned in the ocean surf
and the panic rose and filled my throat
as alone I waited beyond the breakers
treading water
awaiting a fate
that seemed beyond my control

I was rescued then – I need rescue now

Seek First the Kingdom

therefore I tell you
do not worry about your life
seek first the kingdom
seek first the kingdom
seek first the kingdom of God
and his righteousness
and all these things
will be given to you as well
seek first the kingdom

Jesus
You could have had it all
the biggest house
the fastest cars
the most beautiful women
servants and power
financial security
influence and prestige
You were the Boss' Son

instead you chose to put aside the mansion
and the exalted position with all its trappings

instead you chose the peasant girl and her carpenter
a stable floor cleared in the jungle
ruled by a cruel king – a savage barbaric man

instead you chose life as a refugee
and traversed a most inhospitable portion
of your Father's stolen land

no one knew or saw through the disguise
nor could they even begin to comprehend
let alone recognize You....

it can't get much worse
than crucifixion on a Cross of wood and nails
to understand the meaning of suffering and loss
and to be able to entrust all that you are to Another
Your Father
Who then and there chose not to appear

why have you abandoned me
was your excruciated cry
gasped in courageous resolve and despair

so I think you know why I am here
for not nearly as righteous or noble a reason
that you were there
but now You're all I have
and to You
with this badly scrawled note
I entrust all that I hold dear
releasing my hold
I yield to you
timid not bold
in my feeble and tentative way

I have nothing more to say
for silence is all that covers my pain
of letting go and wondering
whether I'll survive tomorrow
or if there'll really be
a resurrection for me

War Vets

many have written of the impact and emotions felt
at their first sight of those aching acres
fertile fields of white crosses
crosses and crosses and more crosses
so many silent witnesses
together and alone
standing with thin arms outstretched

I walked among them in Cambridge
on a warm summer day
thousands of crosses in a white-angled orb
too numerous to count
no dainty daisies were these
casually scattered
to blow and bend in the English breeze
firm and upright
they stood to attention
a stoic and eternal guard of honour
in disciplined formation
neat semi-circular rows
some with names
many without
no one knows who they are
or were
or who they might have been
thousands of young men
faces unseen
from places
God only knows where

around their bases and in-between
grass is clipped and fertile green
and beneath the tranquil surface
you can smell the blood
and begin to count the cost of war
sons and brothers
husbands
fathers
lovers
all lost
and there's a chill in the summer air
as you stare over acres of little wooden sticks
white and bare
and far far beyond
to the boys who died
why

and then there are those who fought
but now live on
with dreams and memories that haunt
from time to time
reminding of past tragedies
that no one else sees or hears
except the one
who bears the scars within
of war and battle fears

and still others
whose marks cannot be hid
for their limbs they gave
not 'cos they were particularly brave
but as an oft' imposed sacrifice
for those who gave orders amidst cigars and gin
many safe miles from where man-made metal
struck the God-made man
in a hell-bent battle for some demonic plan

and now too many
of those brave idealistic and foolish pawns
walk no more
and some can't see
and some can't hear
and some can't feel
and some can't handle
the peace for which
they fought so long

there are no crosses here for them
or for us to find
no tranquil scenes to contemplate
and remind what might have been
just damaged hearts
and shrapnel-shattered minds
and the living wounded
who wheel
limp
and white-cane tap
their battered frames through life
appearing in crooked lines
at Remembrance Day parades
and Legion halls
their distant eyes betray what no word can say
for they never forget or wipe away
the sound and smell of war
the bombs and bullets
the dying crying
thumping grenades
and God knows more

I feel like a war vet myself these days
but all my limbs remain intact
making it hard for you to understand the fact
that minefields explode on the inside too
and wars rage in subtle and subversive ways

at any age or stage of life
causing damage and deep dismay
that takes many days to mend
and comprehend

the challenge facing all who fight
and fall
and bleeding leave the battle site
is knowing how to live from here
how to begin to grow again
accepting the pain of some things never being the same
and hoping to believe one day
that maybe all the suffering
has not been in vain

perhaps
acceptance of unfairness and injustice
as they appear in countless cruel forms
is the key to being reborn

I'm outside Jerusalem again
before a simple Cross
disfigured with Blood and nails
in the shadow of this ancient wall
where the King was hung
a servant saviour flung down
whose humble power tricked death
disabling the dark enemy
with a stunning and unexpected victory

never again would wounds be such
that hope would have to flee
and hence in the light of this stained Tree
I too can rise again with Him
who went to war
for me

Thomas

God
Thomas must have felt so excluded
when he entered the room
and excited friends shouted
guess what happened when you weren't here
Jesus has just appeared
to us

and not to me
he thought
as they continued to chatter and trip over words
describing how frightening and surprising
it was when Jesus walked through the wall
and how Jesus looked
and how they touched Jesus
and what Jesus ate
and how Jesus walked
and how Jesus....

but Thomas couldn't endure any more
his heart and eyes burrowed into the floor
he felt so alone
and cried what about me
how can I believe if I can't see
why Jesus
why didn't You wait for me....
why choose the one time
when I was not there to suddenly appear

and for the next week he endured their speaking
and with anger and doubt hung out on the fringe
and listened alone

just believe
walk by faith
rejoice and don't grieve
let go and let God
trust and receive
how the words cut like a razor-sharp sword
when you question or doubt the ways of the Lord
everything within you wants to say yes
but if you're open and honest
you have to confess that
you're somewhat unsure
if it's true anymore

like Thomas I've wavered
between night and day
feeling left out and forgotten
despite what friends say
enduring those days when hearing's not knowing
and inside I'm doubting while their faith is growing
they testify to new life and I just see death
they rejoice in the morning and I see the darkness increasing
they praise Jesus in songs with joy from on high
I ask in whispers why He passed me by
musing and brooding
I wait in the twilight
darkness still hovers
as doubting and hoping with Thomas I grieve
I want to believe there'll be some reprieve

Jesus I pray,
You'll walk through my walls
and show me Your hands as well
one day

Suffering

what is suffering I, wonder
and who determines whose pain is worse
for it seems to me that one man's blessing
is another man's curse
or what hurts you easily passes me by
and what makes you laugh
brings tears to my eyes

some have called me a prophet
one who speaks out
a voice crying in the wilderness
John the Baptist
one who enjoys 'bucking the system'
and doesn't give a damn about how others feel
offering simplistic solutions
peddling naïve ideals

if only they....

I know the desert road and the prodding weight
of the awkwardness of passionate conviction
when others don't hear how much you care
or feel the beat of your heart
and taste the sweat of your fear
when no one draws near
and only rejection appears in a note from 'them'
saying go you're not welcome here
you're judgmental
dogmatic
insensitive

homophobic
bible thumping
fundamentalist
not diplomatic or compromising

your questioning is rebellion
your non-conformity is anti-authoritarian
your political incorrectness equals lack of respect....

and no one asks or talks
to really find out what you're all about

locusts and honey
camel-hair clothes
sandals
no money
most aren't in vogue
a message from God that's hard to deliver
to a church with no Word
little love and no leader
where the Good Book's been shredded
the prophet's beheaded

A Prayer

Lord melt me back to You
as drips from icy tips
free liquid long imprisoned
at last to run wild and free
in clouds and streams
resurrected soft and new
in the morning dew

Lord let it be like that
melt me back to You
please take this hardness that covers my pain
and the numbness that freezes feelings
drawing me way back inside
like a tortoise hiding within his shell
until all's well once more
with the world

Lord
melt me back to You
restore the trust to believe
that it's no stale crust
You'll toss my way
as I cry out for bread day after day

Lord melt me back to You
show me that You know
where we've been
let my heart beat soft and hard
with Your love
and my voice sing Your songs

from the depth of my soul
send Your Spirit like a dove
on the wings of Your unfathomable love
reassuring this troubled son
who so yearns for....

Lord
melt me back to You
for it's cold in the desert
when the shadows grow long
and the silence drowns out
the sound of the songs
and I can't stay alive out here
watching from afar
I've glimpsed Your presence
and I know of Your kindness
I've been in that place
where I've smelled Your sweet fragrance
and felt You breathing on my face
You've kissed me to life before

I can't keep my distance
and pretend You're not here
I miss You
but I don't know how to return

Anger

it catches me unaware
this anger that flares like a forest fire
sweeping the undergrowth
of my life and actions
exposing every motive
and igniting unresolved matter
strewn across its random path

sometimes that fierce emotion
finds forest fires too tame
and a volcanic eruption is a more apt description
although I seldom explode
but rather simmer
and seep lava down my slopes
letting off pressure and steam
murmuring utter-muttered words
short-fused and bullet-ripped
machine-gun stutters piercing
the unaware with irate verbal salvos

at other times anger flows underground
and the defenses are far less spectacular
nothing heard or too visible
just a minefield of silence

it crawls chameleon-like
flicking a hungry tongue at this and that
ancient rolling eyes slowly swivel
relentlessly searching every kink and flaw

never missing an opportunity to attack
at the slightest hint of weakness

it changes colour and appearance too
sometimes green with jealousy and envy
or blue with despair and depression
hurt and self-pity
maybe gray with numb-bland deadness
and sometimes just plain deep bloody
RED

Up and Down

I can't get over the ups and downs
that relentlessly continue their undulations
between the smiles and frowns of this man
whoever he may be

once I thought that I knew where I was going
and who I was
now I pause to examine the tracks
and discover the circles
in which I have meandered
lead me back to familiar places

I have wandered these shores before
but how I arrived here again eludes me still
what is this spiral of habitation
held together by the invisible
tugging between God and creation
causing endless tension
as together we struggle
the imperfect locked in hand-to-hand combat
with Ultimate Perfection for domination at best
an explanation at worst

who scarred and bruised
and terminally diseased by sin's afflictions
can ever compete on level ground
with such a One Who has no flaw
and in Whom no guile is found

sometimes this man sinful and raw
so disparate and unlike Jesus
feels like a boy in a bubble
and although people are close
the distances appear vast
they make gestures
to which I cannot respond with any coherence
and I make sounds that no one hears
or seems to comprehend

is there no end to this bubbled confusion
in which I presently spiral
revolution after endless revolution
with no fixed place of rest or stillness
how I long for those biblical pastures of grace
where the Shepherd stands guard
never turning His face
from the lion and the lamb at play

Pulling Petals

I drove to Crofton
to the ferry
to silently roll off the ramp
to Saltspring Island in early January

I numbly steered my way to the cabin
and wandered around....

this was where we had dreamed
and built
entertained
and escaped from it all

now it was not far enough
nothing was

there was no destination
or escape from myself
and the gnawing pain was insatiable
a monster with a darkly morbid appetite
and apparently no end to its gluttony

I pace all day
sit
stare at the wall
read a page
walk outside
play music
turn it off
lie down

pick up the guitar
put it down
walk outside
lie down
restlessly fearfully
alone desperately so
desperate

I see the car
and the hose
the duct-tape
the isolation
plenty of time
my children
my wife
my friends – my life

and in the beauty and quietness
of the cabin that mid-winter
after Jesus was born
I pluck the petals of my withered flower
disfiguring its face with my confusion

it was the closest I ever came
to jumping over the brink of a bewildering abyss

in that bleak wasteland of despair
I began to comprehend
how others like me find their way
to this God-forsaken border post
at the edge of the end
and in a snap of time cross over
never to return

I am no longer Judas' judge

Gone Fishin'

gone fishin' just didn't cut it for Peter
the second time around
when he dragged out his nets and boats
for a fishing weekend in Galilee

the whip-crack of sails
stirred his spirit
the boat was meek as a lamb
and strong as a wild horse when
free reined with a galloping wind
and large rolling swells
they worked well together
plying the inland sea
until the nets groaning wet
were heaved aboard
stretched and dripping
fish slithering and slapping tails
silver gray at his feet

it was a life Peter loved
by Tabgha's springs
fishing downwind along Capernaum's shore
silently drifting under stars and rocking lamps
trawling in the dawn's first light
as it blushed behind the hills
rising gentle
later to mature burning hot against a burnished sky
then slowly cool and fall in a dusty ball
behind the western shore

and he knew from the cloud-coloured train
whether tomorrow would bring sun or rain

but
while he could forecast the weather
Simon Peter would never have predicted
the rest of his days
especially that evening
when another Son rose high above his horizon

it had surprised him when the Nazarene
looked him straight in the eye and said
come and follow me

for three years they'd wandered
Christ-crossing lands
leaving all behind he'd changed every plan
and seen things he'd never dreamed could be true
miracles
healing power
love pouring through
to the poor
to the needy
to the Gentile and the Jew

he'd argued and questioned
been baffled and bemused
by Jesus' wisdom and compassion
His rare insight and views
time after time it had made no sense at all
why He did what He did while heeding God's call
opposition had mounted and Peter argued in vain
but Jesus pressed on undaunted and refused to explain

finally Herod
Pilate
and the Sanhedrin

called for blood and the death of the Jew
Peter bravely asserted
Lord I'll never give up or abandon You

but when tested in the garden
like the others he slept
he drew his sword in anger
in the face of a soldier
then a young girl's accusations
left him stuttering denials
that were pathetically lame
and as the cock crowed
he wept with self-loathing and blame

Peter learned of the farcical trial
that later took place
religion can never lose face
Jesus hung on the tree
and Barabbas went free

after such a parting of ways
what do you do
who do you speak to
where do you go
where is there comfort and who understands
the breaking
the nightmares
the nails biting holes in your hands
and remorse in your soul

Simon carried his guilt
down to the tomb
and up into the room
wherever he went it would never relent
which is why he retreated
to Galilee once more

but neither distance nor time
healed the festering sore

even the last night of fishing hadn't fared well
returning tired and weary with nothing to sell
approaching the harbour
they saw a stranger appear
and they wondered who it was
who awaited them there

as the boat drifted closer Peter yelled
it's the Master
it's the Master
and he jumped overboard
and swam to his Lord
soaked to the bone
he stood silent and still
with no words or excuses
to explain his weak will

Simon do you love me,
three times he was asked
yes Lord I love You,
he choked in reply
I can't deny....

then he broke in mid-sentence
humbly expressing in tears
what his words and his actions failed to say
Jesus' response was to embrace his dear friend
bringing the pain of his guilt to a merciful end
a new man was born upon whom He now could depend
and from the shards of rebellion a shepherd was formed
his passion rekindled
his soul strangely warmed
a fisher of men profoundly set free

called again by his Master
to leave Galilee

but this time Simon Peter understood
that he was the servant and Jesus was the Way
he'd never be a potter but always the clay
and he liked it that way

REKINDLED
(PART 2)

"This is my son, whom I love, and in whom I am well pleased."

— (Matt. 3:17)

Love Holds On

peace comes
peace goes
and love holds on

breaking down
straining alone
digging deep
drinking midnight oil
wondering how long
until the treadmill ends
that's when
I need a friend

peace comes
peace goes
and love holds on

when night falls
the wick burns low
day breaks
over a heart that aches

peace comes
peace goes
but love holds on

Loving the Lonely

Jean Vanier, the Catholic Priest who founded the L'Arche Communities for mentally challenged people around the world, describes loneliness and depression in these words:

> I once visited a psychiatric hospital that was a kind of warehouse of human misery. Hundreds of children with severe disabilities were lying neglected, on their cots. There was a deadly silence. Not one of them was crying. When they realize that nobody cares, that nobody will answer them, children no longer cry. It takes too much energy. We cry out only when there is hope that someone may hear us.
>
> Such loneliness is born of the most complete and utter depression, from the bottom of the deepest pit in which the human soul can find itself. The loneliness that engenders depression manifests itself as chaos. There is confusion, and coming out of this confusion there can be a desire for self-destruction, for death. So, loneliness can become agony, a scream of pain. There is no light, no consolation, no touch of peace and of the joy life brings. Such loneliness reveals the true meaning of chaos.
>
> Life no longer flows in recognizable patterns. For the person engulfed in this form of loneliness there is only emptiness, anguish, and inner agitation; there are no yearnings, no desires to be fulfilled, no desire to live. Such a person feels completely cut off from everyone and everything. It is a life turned in upon itself. All order is gone and those in this chaos are unable to relate or listen to others. Their lives seem to have no meaning. They live in complete confusion, closed up in themselves.
>
> – *Becoming Human* (page 9). Jean Vanier – House of Anansi Press – Used with permission.

Don't you find it interesting that God created Eve to be a companion for Adam, insisting that it was not good for him to live alone? God understood that He was 'not enough' for Adam's needs to be fulfilled while living in human form on a finite earth. This is extremely important to comprehend, lest we spiritualize human longings to the point where the acknowledgement of their presence is interpreted as 'something inferior and lesser than'. Insisting that 'all I need is God' indicates some unresolved personal issues in my opinion, rather than evidence of deep spirituality.

I do not believe that human beings have significantly changed through the ages. We are all created to experience comfort and friendship with our fellow human beings through whom God incarnates the reality of love and acceptance. One of the important keys to the healing and recovery from deep depression, I suggest, includes demonstrating unconditional love, acceptance, and validation to the one who is suffering. This is not to be construed to mean that it is necessary to condone all behaviour that is manifest or to agree with every choice that is made. It does mean that it is vitally important to consistently love the person.

Dealing with depression is a complex topic and I do not want to be misunderstood or accused of making overly simplistic statements. In a world where 'MacChristian' and television sound bites happily coexist, the superficial spiritualizing of deep-rooted problems can be devastating and anemically ineffective.

It is not a revolutionary concept to wonder whether the beginning of healing for the depressed person might be similar to that place at which the alcoholic must arrive; a place where at last an acceptance of the reality of the problem or condition is acknowledged. Acceptance introduces at least an openness to consider the potential for change ... and with that hint of possibility the kernel of hope is quietly planted once again. The speed and depth at which hope takes root varies immensely, and within the grasp of my small intellect and comprehension the process remains something of a mystery. However, acknowledging the dilemma and requesting help without the fear of being rejected or dismissed is surely a good place to start? And helpfulness begins by taking the time to listen without pressure to provide some erudite answer. What many people struggling through depression are crying out for is someone to talk to; someone who will take the time to listen carefully and sensitively to them.

After the Fire

I still smell the smoke
wisps of gray spiraling in lazy coils
from the charcoal floor

ancient figures of the earth
stir from a deep sleep
slowly stretching
testing every muscle and limb
before lazily entering awakeness

the terrain is charred
no life is visible on the surface of things

heavenward
the foliage is green though somewhat singed
metamorphosing brown
while down here where I stand
it is black and gray
and ash explodes in puffs of dust
as every heel stepped down
rolls toward the toe
impressing footprints in the ground

the fire has gone
most of the smoke has cleared
but it's still too early for new growth to break through
even though defiant greens prepare
a magnificent resurrection
beneath the black charred earth

I see myself in the smoke
stretching and testing
with those ancient coiling wisps
rising from the hot charred dirt

after the fire
in-between
the black and green burnt foliage
charcoal dreams
awaiting the coming of a new birth....
and the passionate screams of life

Self-pity

self-pity has lurked in my vicinity
for quite some time now
I was going to liken him
to those clichéd well-worn shoes
the pair we tuck away in our closets....
but that seems too homely
too warm and comforting for the likes of him

he's an interesting fellow
sometimes I hardly know that he's here
he blends in so well with the rest of the crowd
congregated around my life

that is until he feels ignored
or passed by
then with slow saunter
blood-hound eyes
and drooping lip that never lifts to smile
he sidles alongside to remind me of his presence
like some mafia hoodlum on a mission for the boss
he whispers in my ear about feelings
reminding me of how we're both so misunderstood
unappreciated abused and taken for granted
and before I know it we walk

he talks – and I agree

feeling his hollow arm around me
as we stroll down the pathway of least resistance
is no comfort at all

it offers no warmth
yields no compassion
rather – it's a damp and cold chaffing on my shoulders
like an old yoke weighing down heavy
but still disturbingly familiar

if I'm not careful I can entertain him for hours
even offer hospitality for days
because although I hate to admit it
I can enjoy his company and his sullen ways
as he stokes my grief and dolefully empathizes
with my unfair state dealt by the fate he loves to hate

eventually even I have had enough
but when I rise to leave
he clings like a leach in a muddy pond
and sucks with parasitic desperation

my newfound anger and contempt rise up
I shake him off
slam the door and exit
cursing that I've been seduced once more

Faith, Hope, Love

faith hope and love

now there's a trio whose presence
will send self-pity scurrying from center stage
like a cockroach trapped in the unexpected
glare of a spotlight

I haven't seen them much of late
but in recent days I've heard their laughter
and now and then have glanced their way
and realized how much I've missed their company

I used to find their presence difficult to handle
and their incessant optimism naïve and hard to bear
I would mutter under steamy breath
words clouded in gloom
about superficiality
and how they didn't understand the feelings of death
or the power of darkness
with the crushing ache of despair as it breaks
the heart and torments the mind

but one day when we gathered together
and talked a while I saw....

love's distorted hands
scarred and scabbed
gloved in blood

faith's eyes
deep with wisdom
filled with images of things still unseen

hope standing
not flighty or weak at all
but powerful in build and solid in stance

I realized then
that they knew me only too well
and could understand
the meaning of much more
than mere created things

hope surprised me the most
as no wishful dreamer
but one who spoke with confidence and pride
of the One who sustains all three
in times when they like me
would rather flee
in fact they knew far more profoundly than I
about how to live and how to die

how do you do it
was my question
in the face of their peace and teasing optimism

first said love
we know the One above
and then said faith
we believe He truly hears and cares
which is why we're sure
added hope
that we can endure and cope through thick and thin
besides they cried linking arms in unison
we're tough to beat when unified

without faith and hope said love
I'd be like a wounded dove
fearfully flapping wings and limping
on the ground with mournful sound

I can't exist alone
and I hate whistling in the dark
I need love and faith was hope's reply
to help me not succumb to satan's lie
for it's on their thermals
that I with eagle's wings do fly
boldly soaring and riding high

and I faith sighed would never get by
without love and hope as friends by my side
to remind me of those truths unseen
unchanging and eternal and for ever being

so why do I feel so alone I cried

you needn't be
we'll keep you company

but know this they whispered
with soft hushed breath
we rejoice in life
because we're unafraid of death
we've been all the way with the Father's Son
to hell and back and then some
we've tested that of which we speak
and you'll find out too
that we'll be strong when you are weak

but don't be fooled
it's not ourselves in whom we trust
nor do we within ourselves contain
the power to overcome such pain

it's to Him we look
who on the Cross released us to you at such a cost
and in His Blood He wrote your name with ours entwined
so that defeat will never again twin with despair
conspiring to make you a slave to doubt and fear

but rather in His victory we do arise
and are made new in you
bringing life to truth
and death to lies

Being There

A motivating factor for me to write about depression has been to 'get it out of my system'. As I was enduring the experience writing was the only way I could find to try and put into words what I was experiencing within. It is my hope that maybe in a small way some of these words will encourage one who struggles with depression, or who feels orphaned and lonely deep within their spirits. It is an attempt to give a voice to the incompleteness present in all of us (in various measure) but unacknowledged, dismissed, or denied by many.

The institutions I was raised in never admitted to such frailties. Leadership derived authority from roles and rules rather than *from people* in leadership positions modelling humility, transparency, and interdependence. Instead of honestly and healthily demonstrating how to embrace human frailty (a facet of every personality and human being), leadership was by and large modelled by those who attempted to hide or deny their weaknesses.

I have always been more encouraged to learn how wounded people live in hope, than to hear how an intellect defends untested theories. I'm talking about the following examples of 'inner secrets'....

Longing for a fulfilment that so far has eluded you in your lifetime and you wonder whether you'll ever find 'it'.

Passionately and sincerely following the Christian way (or maybe some other spiritual journey) and yet ... when you are quiet and alone there is still an ache and an emptiness; and to acknowledge that will sound like a lack of faith or failure (both false conclusions in my opinion).

Appearing to be strong and relatively successful, while inside you're experiencing a rumbling of what feels like a looming emotional avalanche and you're just trying to hold on as best you can – but there's no one to talk to! So you keep busy, pray, sing, work, read, work, play, parent; just keep on keeping on ... and people are so grateful for all you contribute ... can't let the cat out of the bag now!

Growing up within the confines of rigid belief systems that you 'almost' willingly embrace. However, as you have grown older, whenever you have wanted to test or challenge what is just 'accepted' – it has been difficult to know where or how to do that without being rejected, misunderstood, or threatened in some manner. Therefore you quietly withdraw into yourself and no one knows ... or ... you move right out, rebel and lose everything ... and still do not find peace or understanding.

These are places that feel so immature, self-pitying and vulnerable at times; and to question or give expression to such realities is to possibly betray friendships and risk rejection, dismissal, or ridicule. Which is why it's tempting to discount their validity and even easier to bury them under mounds of busyness, good works, or angry denial.

The greatest gateway to the healing of emotional pain is to be found in the expression and acknowledgement of its existence in the first place. If you're extremely fortunate, you may receive genuine validation from a significant person who responds with non-judgemental acceptance and a willingness to continue to 'be there' for you.

Quite frankly I have always found responses without engagement to be insulting and simplistic. Anyone can quote the Bible or advocate making choices, blame the devil, or prattle off some well-worn cliché. Invariably those responses meet the needs of the dispenser rather than provide encouragement for the one who is struggling. That does not mean that the principles conveyed in the Bible, or the makings of choices, etc., are irrelevant. What I am talking about is the 'tone of voice used' to convey perceptions, truths, or suggested remedies and solutions.

In the Biblical accounts of Jesus' interaction with people there is a constant juxtaposition between the quality and integrity of His responses and those of the religious leaders. The religious people spoke with harsh tones, absolutes, and a blatant lack of love and compassion. In seeking to further their perceived purpose of God (which invariably was conveniently intertwined with their own positions of authority and power) they neglected the heart of God.

Jesus, on the other hand, loved people first and then led them to embrace the eternal truths of God. His tone of voice was entirely different to that of the religious leaders. He was neither surprised nor upset by the revelation that people are quite naturally 'sinful and rebellious', and that they tend to look for fulfillment in all the wrong places. He revealed truth by shining light, expressing unconditional love, and modeling (or incarnating) *another way of being human*. He refused to berate the darkness by attempting to whip others into compliance within a system (religion-o'-nine-tails) to which He did not submit. Neither did He, in the name of compassion, jettison the truth for the sake of expedience or political correctness. He was never one to look to polls, moneylenders, or lobbyists for affirmation or confirmation of anything. I suspect He would have had just as controversial a relationship with religious leaders today as He did when He first walked this troubled earth. It's all about power and who is ultimately in charge; an issue that surfaced at the beginning of creation when the serpent slithered into Eden and then later attempted to coil around Jesus' will in the wilderness.

There have been many occasions when I have wanted to push aside someone else's pain because I have not known what to do with it. None of us enjoys a sense of lost helplessness and yet, for those who struggle with despair, possibly the greatest gift that can be shared is not a solution or a tool to fix 'their problem', but rather a loving and deeply compassionate presence.

Being with a person – without an agenda, and seeking nothing in return. Communicating that they are loved and precious (not always with words) because of who they are, because God loves them, delights in them, and looks upon them as His beloved. Nothing we do, or anyone else for that matter, will change the reality of God's unconditional love for every human being. However, our words and actions are quite capable of spoiling the view, and we can unwittingly block the sun/Son and deprive another of entering into an experience of that truth by our demeanor in the name of God.

I've often found the example of our own human feelings of love for another person to be a helpful analogy in understanding something of the reality of God's love for us. I invite you to participate in this simple reflective exercise to help get in touch with that reality at a gut level:

Think for a moment about the person whom you love more than anyone else in the world (pause): *feel that feeling* deep within your being, see them in your mind's eye (don't rush).

Think and feel what you wish and desire for that person, your response when they do wrong, your response when they come before you and apologize or seek your help. It's not hard to extend mercy to them, is it?

Do you show them mercy? Do you defend them when others criticize them?

Now try to comprehend this truth revealed quite uniquely through Jesus alone: the astounding fact that *God 'feels' the same way about you* ... except so much more. He likes you, He loves you, and He delights in you – even before you realize it, understand it, or are prepared to accept it.

I used to ask people to tell me about the God whom they reject and do not believe in. I would invariably agree with them and state that I also did not believe in such a god. They never described Him to me in terms of One who loved them within the context of a personal relationship; because they had never encountered Him like that, as He had revealed Himself through Jesus. The God they rejected was invariably locked up in church, religion, a bad childhood experience, or the academic abstraction responsible for all the war and suffering – you know the story.

"As I have loved you – love one another." If God had not revealed His love through the person of Jesus Christ, we would never know that He is personal and loves us. Without such a revelation we are stuck with the conclusions arising from our extremely limited perspective and worldview – because surveying the scene from where we stand we can only conclude the world is chaotic. It would be like trying to rationally surmise that the world and its inhabitants are beautiful and clean if one's only exposure was from living on a garbage dump and never seeing beyond that stench and filth.

Suffering, brokenness, cruelty, injustice, famine, war, abuse, exploitation, disillusionment – all these factors make it impossible for us to logically believe that God is love and that He cares about the world. God understands such a reality and therefore graciously offers us another perspective of Himself; a perspective given through revelation (a knowledge that cannot be logically deduced from our vantage point but instead requires external input).

The Christian believes that this knowledge and understanding entered history in the person of God's Son in the incarnation of Jesus. An event that is more believable precisely because it appears at first glance to be so ridiculously unbelievable. Through the person of Jesus we are given an exquisite and quite unique glimpse into the heart of God. Through His life, death, and resurrection we learn something of His view of the world and of our purpose in it; and of His astounding response to suffering, brokenness, and even depression and despair.

Being with ... and allowing to be – returning again and again – such actions and attitudes speak more to me of the fact of love than any words uttered. In my darkest days there were some, not many, who were there for me in that manner. Later they would tell me how scared they were by the lack of expression in my eyes and the despair in my countenance. What a compliment to them that they were able to continue to walk by my side when I offered so little appreciation and response in return. I am eternally grateful to those who could look past my actions and embrace the broken boy who had become so incredibly lost and vulnerable.

In the final analysis there are no presidents, CEOs, or pastors, no beauty queens or shining knights, no paragons of virtue – no roles at all imparting worthiness and stature in the eyes of God. There are just ordinary people making their way through life as best they can. Some people enjoy wonderful breaks of fortune; some get few.

There are no 'clean saints' in history. Up close all of us are ordinary human beings, with a few who may have been fortunate enough to accomplish some things extraordinarily well. Life has never been about being perfectly good according to my relative frame of reference. It is about developing a relationship with our Creator who is perfectly good and trustworthy, and then in trying to live according to His frame of reference (which is not a straitjacket of religious rules dousing every spark of enjoyment in life). Therein lies the key to greatness and fulfillment both in this world and for eternity.

The problem with depression, it seems to me, is that it is 'almost' an honest place, where the idealism of faith meets the reality of experience. The deception of depression is that the 'blackness and despair' is true reality, and that the overwhelming feelings experienced are the basis of that truth. Without the introduction of some reason to hope in a truth that is beyond my self and my subjective feelings (a more objective foundation upon which faith with integrity is based) there is no reliable counterbalance. Somehow these various aspects of reality have to make peace with one another in order that a richer future may emerge from the ashes.

Depression for me was like living in a godless, meaningless, hopeless universe, where I was abandoned and alone. When one is disillusioned and despairing, even of God's love and care, it is even more vital that those who claim to serve Him reach out. My experience was that most leaders I talked with did not know what to do with me and were singularly ill-equipped to reach out. They appeared to be uncomfortable and uneasy with the awkward failings of one of their peers. The vast majority quickly fell silent and withdrew when the situation invited them to give of themselves as fellow human beings rather than remain safely tucked behind a 'religious role'. I poured my heart out to many and invariably wished I had not been so vulnerable after they hugged me and walked away, never to return. I felt very abandoned and increasingly cynical.

Peace

the inlet ripples liquid ink
lapping logs and stones
etched lamplight
blinking reflections
between rolling hills
and across the night silence stirs
leaving undisturbed the sleeping birds

these nomadic gulls are quiet and content
as they gently rest upon their watery nest
fretting not 'bout what the morrow brings
for as long as they their company keep
they float secure in their drifting
and in their sleep

I hear God speak
of how for every feather and hair
He a record keeps
so watch and learn
from lessons floating on the tide
be still in Him
and in His love abide

River

I've read of sailors
who have plied long voyages across wide oceans
without glimpse of land nor hint of ground
and when at last there is coast to explore
they can sense the shore long before
their eyes spy vegetation rising
from that spindly distant line
where sea and sky do meet

in Africa
there are times when
one can smell the rain approaching
before the sky grows clouds
and big wet drops
splash craters in the mud

with God
I think it's sometimes like that as well
you can sense Him when definition has not yet formed
and before understanding and faith drench your soul

I have been a dry sponge
a broken cistern
a river bed of fractured clay and crumbling dust
no moisture in sight
no hint of a cloud
just memories of water that used to flow
between these scarified barren banks of crusty furrows
bearing witness

to what once was but now no longer is
and today cracks with gasping sorrow

a shell on the shore placed to the ear
captures the ocean's roar
yet no life appears from that hollow cave
and what was once a home
is now an empty grave

at last I think I hear thunder
and I see the clouds building
swelling and bloating over the vistas of my being
deep within my spirit I smell the rain
and with ear pressed to the dust of this desolate bed
I sense movement in the hills
as rivulets scurry down their ancient paths
and I hold my breath
could this nightmare drought be at an end
and my river begin to bend and flow once more

I close my eyes and dream of banks of green
with grass and ferns and birds that sing and bounce-hop
between trees that grow wild and strong
deep rooted hoisting luscious fruit
high up to the heavens

I'm alive again
the gravestone's rolled away
and joy has filled this day
drinking deep
water beads down leaf and skin
mingled with tears that flow
from those deep wells so mysteriously unplumbed within

and hope
even one drop that falls upon my brow
gives hint I trust of what is yet to come

South Africa

South Africa in 1952 was a country straining under the policies of discrimination and oppression imposed by the relatively new Nationalist government. The grand scheme hatched by Afrikaner dreamers and idealists was based upon their misguided conviction or rationalization that God never intended races to mix. As with most other misguided visions deep wounds still festering from past defeats and abuses also distorted them.

The Nationalists understood their mission as a messianic calling and a mandate to establish a land where *they* could grow and flourish as a culture and as a nation. The fact that this vision trampled upon the rights and aspirations of others was never understood as an inconsistent portrayal of Biblical teaching. Thus the most awful human cocktail was mixed even before the stench and dust of the gruesome Nazi experiment in Europe had settled. In fact, for many on that Southern tip of Africa the German vision inspired and intoxicated them with thoughts of their own glorious future; rather than sobering them with an insight into the blind stupidity humanity is capable of inflicting upon its own. South Africa in the early fifties was firming up the foundations of Apartheid.

The madness would culminate in Black rights being allocated to homelands while Black muscle was harnessed in the cities to drive the White economic machine. Blacks were the servants and Whites were the masters and madams; Blacks lived in poor and dirty conditions outside the cities and towns; Whites lived in suburbs with 'servant's quarters' in the back where the maids existed as best they could. Blacks swept the streets, collected garbage, worked on the roads and railways – Whites put out the garbage, sat in the first-class 'Whites Only' sections of the trains, and drove their cars along the highways. White children had Black nannies while mothers played tennis and drank tea with friends. Black children didn't wear shoes, and sometimes sold newspapers at traffic lights until late at night. Black children went to bed hungry (slept on the floor) and maybe saw their mothers once a week when they came home for a day off from their White employers.

Many Black children lived with their mothers and grandparents in rural areas while their fathers worked in the cities. These men formed the resource known as 'migrant labour'. They lived alone in what amounted to army barracks in townships. They endured because they had to, possibly with the hope of travelling home to their families and children maybe once a year.

I never mixed with Black people on a peer level during the first twenty years of my life; such was the tragic effectiveness of apartheid. Caricatures, myths, and prejudices thrive on ignorance and 'separate development'. I've found that fact to be true on every continent and in every culture where I have lived.

We are different and yet so much is the same. Prejudice thrives when people never meet, listen, or share a meal together.

Crash-site

what must I do
what must I do
what must I do
be still
be still
be still

stay with the wreckage is the first command
given to those who crash in the back of beyond
don't wander too far
don't leave the site
rescue will come
be patient – sit tight
it's a basic rule to survive
wait and be still and you'll get out alive

as I survey these past months
things easy to say have been hard to apply
when you're buckled up in pain
to be told to be patient and still
is an infuriating refrain

Jesus sleeps
and His servants aren't sure
of the right remedy or the cure
they make one phone-call
one inquiry
and then they're gone
preferring to preach to the lost
then walk alongside the 'wounded found'

indeed for some 'wounded found'
is a contradiction in terms
I wonder how long this takes
will there ever be a day
when I don't feel the ache of a life and spirit shattered
like Humpty's head splattered after the fall
strangely
in the stillness and the resting in being
angels have come unheard and unseen
awakening a flickering hope
which I don't understand
and healing once again warms the blood
of my being – ever so slightly

Wind

the Arctic wind blew over the hills last night
an icy chill
that whipped white horses
across the back of the bucking inlet
and bullied my clothes while I paced the shore
knifing sadistically with cold stabs
piercing every layer of cloth and skin
until it had penetrated
all of my frail humanity and
I shivered uncontrollably

in the teeth of such mocking
there was nothing else to do
but take refuge
in the shelter of another place
where warmth gently thawed me
back to life again
that bitter wind blowing biting
cutting through the air
reminds me of the critical spirit
that relentlessly attacks behind the back
magnifying every flaw and crack
then disappears innocent
when deep despair appears

so unlike the warm breeze that blows
when Jesus stands outside our human tomb
and says
roll away the stone

despite the protestations of some
who exclaim that it stinks in there

meanwhile inside I wait with Lazarus for grace
and listen to those outside discuss my fate
until my eyes are blinded by flooding light
the barrier's removed
and the fresh breeze sings
come out upon its wings
my heart revives and hope soars
choosing life once more
I shuffle through death's dark gloom
across the floor and from the tomb
to stand in the open
exposed and weak
alive again but still unable to speak
friends are there
spectators too
some shocked
some surprised
all unsure of what to do

then He speaks

take off the grave clothes
unbind my friend
as I have loved you....
so are you to love him too

Music and my Early Church

One of my earliest recollections of 'church' is of my father taking us to St. Paul's Anglican Church in Rondebosch, Cape Town. Situated on the slopes of the mountain that towers over the southern suburbs (ironically called Devil's Peak) the church stands on a small hill surrounded by trees. It is built of warm rusty brown and yellow sandstone and is quite large and imposing; particularly when viewed through the eyes of a seven-year-old boy. When little boys walked through the arched doors of St. Paul's they were unsure of whether they were entering a dungeon, a palace, or a castle.

Inside the church soaring buttresses and beams lift a peaked roof up to the heavens. The windows rise majestically, filtering God's light through magnificent stained-glass scenes depicting biblical themes of shepherds, and prophets, and truths of another world. Closer to earth reality is more harsh; the seats are solid and hard, wooden, and rigidly placed row after row like trenches to be occupied by soldiers engaging and preparing for battle. Prayers are prayed on knees cushioned by kneelers and one can spend a lot of time crouched on them desperately trying to look 'as if you mean every word'.

Strange words are spoken from musty books in the kind of English that little boys don't begin to understand. The organ plays and its mighty sound rolls around like a giant's pinball bouncing off the sides of the chiseled sandstone and pounding into young unappreciative ears. The procession begins with choir and robes and candles and singing. The priest enters last in line with his Pinocchio nose tilted upward singing sonorously as he slowly follows the other 'lesser beings', the fringes of his ornate vestments silently sweep the marble floor around him. Finally, on arrival at the altar, which seems very far away, he stops and bows, turns and speaks to no one in

133

particular – the service has begun while little boys are already wondering when it will end.

The words read and the hymns sung tell of Jesus, who was humble and easy to come close to – One who loved children and did not frighten them. The stain-glass windows depict this same One caring for people. Boys and girls are perched upon His knee or nestle into His broad shoulders, a lamb is cradled in His arm; there's no fear or distance there. But nothing in what I experience in this vast place speaks of warmth and love and the humble invitation of a shepherd for His sheep to come to Him without delay. Instead it feels like I've entered the guardhouse of a King who is very distant and serious and the guards/clergy will determine who comes in, when and how.

That guardhouse was to become a familiar place throughout my childhood and teenage years. School, church, and chapel all seemed to be like that – where God was spoken of and sung about and read about – but despite all the rhetoric He was never present in a personal capacity to meet and to know and talk to. On the other hand the guards were always present, front and centre, blocking the view to heaven.

Between the age of six and thirteen I sang as a treble in the boy's choir, attended multitudes of church services but was never introduced to the Jesus who loved me personally. I sang the treble solo in Faure's Requiem ... Pie Jesu Domine, and participated in mass choirs performing in the Cape Town City Hall works of Handel's Messiah, Belshazzar's Wedding Feast, and countless hymns and carols. The aesthetic beauty of the music was celebrated and applauded and I was thrilled to be part of the grandeur of it all.

However, all I heard of the One about Whom most of the music was written and composed was that He was to be respected and revered. It was only when I attended a youth group in a little Methodist Church called Mossop Hall at the age of thirteen that I was introduced to a personal God. A light of meaning and revelation went on for me when I discovered that He was not like the priests after all, and that He had revealed Himself surprisingly informally and yet wonderfully in the person of Jesus His Son. And Jesus, the carpenter, was more likely dressed in denim and an open-neck shirt speaking the colloquial language, than adopting the affected role of a religious leader. It was such a refreshing and exciting revelation!

The problem then was that I had to constantly juggle my allegiances between devotion and love for God, and the fact that I liked going to church because the girls were there. That is quite another story....

Sunday Morning

it's been almost a year
since I sat in despair at the airport
where every day and night people pass through
embracing countless hello's and good-bye's
tears and laughter
arrivals and departures
endings and beginnings

I wrote with such trembling fear of my disintegrating life
where all form and sense had vaporized
before my eyes

1997 did not bring much soaring flight
but rather buckled the plates of my life's crust once more
shaking the foundations and rattling the rafters
of all that had come before
valleys opened
vast chasms of deep depression
grand canyons of introspection and eroded self-esteem

the mountains of hope and friendship
lining my sides for months on end
provided little comfort
instead they were more like tall
overwhelming prison walls
than hands that helped and coaxed me upward
to somehow attain
the tantalizing Shangri-la called freedom

through that dark crevasse
a mere crease in the earth's old and wrinkled skin
I journeyed where many have trod before
though each pilgrim
inevitably feels they are the first
to explore and experience
the pangs of insatiable hunger
and such a deep and bitter thirst

trudging through the muddy damp within
walking weary day by day
stumbling at night
sometimes snatching troubled and restless sleep
I sought my answers
invariably intertwined with questions
that clung like tumbleweed to my tired reason

I had thought I wanted meaning
or maybe just another way to make sense and explain
the shimmering mirage of my confused reality
and by the path my family fell
tired of the hell I'd led them through
work was sacrificed upon this altar of discontent
and by year's end
I lived alone
refusing
nay
rather struggling to know
how to repent

today I sit in a rented cottage
typing at a table fifty yards from the ocean

this January Sunday
is quiet
the air is cold and clear
it's a winter morning

hardly a cloud has appeared across the ice-blue sky
the sun continues its circumnavigation of every human
   horizon
the sea is calm
ripples break ranks and march
in flat regimented lines from sea to shore
if I stand outside I can hear their swooshing arrival on the
   beach
but this morning they're no more intimidating
than are children playing soldiers' games in a war of
   makebelieve

from my window I watch the waves advance
along this coastal shore
as they have
for more years than I can comprehend
beyond in the distance are the
hazy gray mainland mountains under big skies
I focus on the mountains
the snow and sun appear to delight in each other's company
deftly creating a collage of exquisite colours
draped and poured over the gigantic formations
or enfolding the outstretched limbs of a tree
that I imagine but do not see

along this shoreline
ducks bob in peaceful unison
on liquid-cool steel blue tranquility
frost icing the logs scattered along the beach
slowly melts
and trickles down their wooden sides
like sweat or tears on weathered cheeks

it's a beautiful place

yesterday
I walked along this shore at the turn of the tide

'bout half-an-hour before a dark
that never really came
because the moon was nearly full
and the heavens almost clear

as daylight dimmed
a shimmering path of threadbare yellow
rolled out across the bay
and those same bobbing ducks of yesterday
were silhouetted black weaving back and forth
down the moon's watery road
like some amiable drunks reluctant to leave a party
and unsure of where to go to next

I took some photographs as a memory and
thought I might paint from them some day
I watched an eagle settle in the shallows
for an evening meal of fresh shellfish
graciously delivered on a sandy platter
by a acquiescent tide

an ocean
sometimes so gentle and hospitable
generously catering to those
who wade and live along her shores
yet at other times unwilling to yield anything without a fight
and to give no more than is wrested and tugged
from her undulating breast

she's always been that way
the one who calls the tune
and decides when to yield
and when to share
what to reveal and what to hide
fickle yet magically mesmerizing
she insists on being shown respect
and jealously guards her reputation

of being slightly unpredictable
and when she flirts with the moon
she goes wild

how many birds have flown
and fed and swum along these shores
I wondered
catching meals and breaking shells
day after day
year after year

it's a beautiful place

and I'm glad to be here
landing like any other migrating bird in need of rest and food
taking time to float and feed
before continuing on a journey of uncertain destination

for now I'll join the ducks
and enjoy their unthreatening company
trying to learn from them
the joy of being in one place through every season
without frantically flapping and flying
in the migrants' restless race
chasing from place to place
an eternal summer
someone watching
might think I'm also just another amiable drunk
paddling in the moonlight
and they may well be right
for I admit I am treading water
and wondering where to go....

but it's a beautiful place
to wait and to watch
and to maybe learn a thing or two
and even be confused....

Winter Storm

the ducks
those bobbing drunks
of whom I spoke the other day
must be in hiding tonight
for the weather is foul
(no pun intended)
the sea – no longer calm and placid in the bay
tosses and flicks long wet strands of iridescent spray
every which way
she's wild and irritable

it's hardly surprising really
because the wind is behaving like a rebellious teenager
swerving between cottages and trees and
careening out over the ocean with destructive abandon
it's a night to be protected and sheltered
and warmed at the hearth
a night for souls to be shielded
from the mocking taunt of the wind
and where a dwelling is a good place to be
a warm refuge

there comes a time
like now
when words decline the invitation to speak
and lips are vacant and hollow
mouthing empty shapes bereft of sound

ride out the storm however you may
turn your back on the wind

turn your back on the rain
turn your stone-cold face
toward the fire and the flame
and let their fingers gently caress
with shadows inducing sweet rest

but whatever words I choose
neither shelter nor fire or the poems I peruse
can ever replace the profoundly deep need
for the emotion – the presence
of a most human embrace and a friendly face
nothing else can impart love's warmth to the heart
and therein is the place
truly – to shelter from storms

what I'm really trying to say is
I'm lonely

Saturday Phone Call

I looked after the children this weekend
swapped accommodation
because it worked out more conveniently
that's why I wasn't expected to be home
on Saturday afternoon when the phone rang

when I answered
silence responded from the other end
silence when I said hello
silence to my repeated greeting

the anonymous 'other' breathed quiet
waiting for me to hang up
it was like conversing with death
in a place where living words once overflowed
I dialed 'last caller'
and a machine bridged the vacuum revealing the one
who with such muted eloquence had spoken volumes
I recognized the name
I knew them well
but what the hell
they're also angry and hurting

it's still hard to live with though

so I choose the cocoon
the self-blown bubble into which I withdraw
trying to ignore the sound of the slamming
and the sight of closing doors

the previous night someone else had called
and spoken in a politely bland official tone
like a stranger pretending not to know
so cool and distant
communicating judgement in an instant
we've all done it
or maybe I'm just hyper-sensitive

Christians speak of unconditional love
a wonderful ideal that's tough to apply
a Pharisee not I we flatly deny
yet still travel with hands clutching stones
and eyes filled with wood
dead men's bones walking by
we sing the songs of Jesus
to drown the groans of the wounded and falling
we give bread to the stranger and preach to the sinner
but deliver the cold shoulder to the brother or sister
who should have known better
we whisper and mutter

all I need is a bell or maybe a gong
to pound like a leper as I walk through the streets
singing my unclean song

when you live on the wrong side of the track
and struggle to get back 'they' give looks and stares
and sometimes behave as if you're not there
for in my past as a holy physician
to stumble and fall and show weakness at all
was not good and is certainly a reality not understood

you can speak of being weak and teach about sin
mercy and grace and the demons within
but if you ever give in and your hand loses hold
mercy's withdrawn and grace turns judge-cold
this state of being separated

is an awkward place of in-between indecision
partly in and partly out
striking a match
but not quite ready to burn the bridge
looking back at the past
squinting at the future
peering through the unfamiliar fog of the present

I give awkward cries for help
usually through actions even as simple
and mundane as answering the phone
the receiver clicks into place
like a slap in the face
silence resumes drowning grace

who'll ring next is anyone's guess
but maybe I won't answer again for a while

Hands Without Stones

one day those hands would bleed
rivers of scarlet from writhing fingers
pinned to wood with rough-nailed cuffs
grasping and clawing in agonized futility
seeking relief from the gnawing demons of judgement day

they would hang 'til lifeless limbs no longer breathed nor bled
this One
of Whom some said
there was no reason for making Him be dead like this
betrayed by a kiss

but then He marched to another plan
penned by One
infinitely more grand than those before whom He'd stand
upon this earth
and whose petty justice and stupid grandeur
would sentence Him to a death of which they knew nothing

and finally after Cross and Stone were set in place
God bridged the rift with shattering grace
and by His own creative hand that bloody corpse did lift
from grave to heaven
perfectly redeeming His beloved and vandalized gift

but before that time and while still here
there was a day when those same hands came uninvited near
and reached out quite unexpectedly to me
despite rebukes from the righteous ones at His side

whose venomous words stung like the spit
of fork-tongued snakes hissing in a loveless pit

His were the only silent empty hands among that busy crowd
    of men
shouting religiously about this woman they'd bravely snared
and caught in the very act – of adultery
drooling like hunters' hounds baying over their foe
at last run down and brought to ground
they strut and squawk
so proud of capturing one devoid of any hope of escape
and who now must endure the agony of their judicial rape

blind guides blind hunters
blind Pharisees gather to press the charge
and vindicate themselves before God and one another
can it really be true
that one man's sense of righteousness is bought at another's
    expense
a bargain struck under the whimpered confession of sinfulness
face down in the dust
guilty I writhed naked
surrounded by men whose hands clutched stones
as hard as their hearts
ready to break the bones in a body they had once caressed
at least with lingering eyes that
hid secrets they would never dare confess

and no one asked about the man
we never saw his face
while I was dragged and cornered in that square
they let him slip away from there
it didn't seem quite fair
but then who cares

thank God
there was the One whose mouth had not moved

in unison with the company He kept
and whose eyes
looking not like other men
gazed deep within to read my soul
and comprehending that which I had never known
wept at what was written there
His gentle hands hung still
then slowly stooped and scratched
in snake-pit sand with bent-fingered quill
until
there was no sound
save the breathing and crying
of the living and the dying

strangely silent angrily calm
He rose
and by my huddled side
looked each man in the eye
with a gaze
from which there was no escape

if you have no sin then you be the first to throw a stone

not one man said a word
nor looked they again into his face
such was their disgrace when He had held their soul
within that brief eternal glance
each lowered their guilty eyes
and dropped their stones meekly at His feet
then walked slowly
out of the view of He whom they now knew
had read the soiled pages of their hearts too
He placed His hand upon my brow
crushed under the weight of the damned
whose cry has no hope of being heard
and sinks in shame without voice or name
assuming every blame

and He spoke my name
with words of comfort
words of mercy
words of challenge
as a father with his favourite child would converse
and I drank greedily from His proffered cup
His unassuming love slaked my deepest thirst
as I received from those brave hands
a gift that richly clothed my soul and limbs
with a fabric softly woven
in a forgiving love no coin could ever buy
save that which He for me
one glorious and awful day would choose to pay
when He too was dragged naked into a square
and for a while at least it seemed no one was there for Him
except the savage beast

'twas not the shouts of righteous men
that turned my life around
but the gentle touch of a dusty hand
stretched out to this poor leper on the ground
that told me I was found

'twas not their voice spoke truth to me that day
but His I heard in heart and soul
before He'd even uttered a word
conviction comes in mysterious ways
to receive the truth that He conveys

oh how much we hinder
interrupting what He'd say
quick pouncing every sinner
and lecturing with pecking hands
like squawking birds of prey

but when those hands reach out in love
slowly the fellow sinner faltering stands

at first so unsteady on the ground
and hand in hand we both begin to learn
to walk again
together

Cape Town

Winter at the southern tip of Africa is when the wind blows from the north and the rain drapes wet veils across Table Bay until the mountains are smudged in dark clouds. But in the summer, when the south wind blows and the sea reflects sky-blue and bottle green, the same mountains rise regal, clear and proud.

Across the bay glistening black rocks protrude like ancient teeth from the white sands of Blaaubergstrand (Blue Mountain Beach), and when viewed from this vantage point Table Mountain rises strong, serene, and unbelievably picturesque. I never tired of admiring her through the foam-lace-spray of breaking surf tossed ashore by a powerful Atlantic. Three thousand feet of granite and sandstone, sides scored and scarred by millennia of erosion, support a summit that rests long and flat like a giant's table by the sea.

On her left (as I look at her) is Devil's Peak, a more traditionally sculptured mountain whose slopes are adorned with forests and trails and places to roam. Baboons live in packs and chatter in the trees as deer pick their way quietly between long slender Cape pines and silver-leaf trees. In the background one can hear the low drone while Cape Town works and plays, but on these slopes it is also possible to be far away and find refuge in the view and solace of the mountain.

A mountain pass separates Table Mountain's right side from gently undulating hills that, to the imaginative eye, resemble the shape of a vigilant lion at rest. The majestic head and mane of shaggy rock (Lion's Head) flows down a ridge to the smooth rump of Signal Hill. This 'rump' protects Sea Point and the surrounding areas from the buffeting southwesterly that rakes the coast every summer. All three mountain slopes merge down toward the sea where they form the basin that has cradled Cape Town for the past four centuries.

Cape Town's coastline curves in a graceful crescent away from Table Mountain, the harbour, and the 'Castle' built by early settlers, past the Cape Flats, where industry and much of the population dwells, to sweep ever northward. It snakes up the endless beaches of white sand, through the flowers that set the land aflame with colour every spring; traverses the mouth of the mighty Orange river where countless tons of earth are moved and the bedrock is swept clean in search of the diamonds that make men crazy and women swoon. It does not step there but presses on into the choking dust and moving dunes of the Namibian desert, through war-torn Angola, up into the very heart of Africa herself.

Extending southward behind Table Mountain is a long crooked backbone of hills and ridges baptised by the colonialists with English names: Twelve Apostles, Elephant's eye, Silvermine, and Radar Hill. The mountains skirt Simonstown and Smitswinkelbay, and taper off at Cape Point, where they culminate as cliffs that dive steeply into the crashing surf twenty-five miles south of Cape Town. Along the foothills of this 'backbone' villages have emerged over the centuries to house those who have harvested the abundance of fish found in the convergence of the Atlantic and Indian oceans. Now, however, the coast has fewer fish and many more houses. They cluster like loosely strung necklaces of muscles and barnacles along the lower mountain slopes just above the high-tide line and the railway tracks, stretching almost continuously from Cape Town to Cape Point. These are the 'southern suburbs'.

I was born in the southern suburbs on this crooked gnarled tip of a continent of infinite beauty with vast spaces of mountains to climb and oceans to swim in. One can dive into the Atlantic and swim in the Indian ocean on the same day, within one hour.... It's a land that grips your heart and never lets go. A land that also straddles the 'first' and 'third' worlds in a precarious balancing act that unfortunately became tragically unglued.

Another reality in Cape Town was of a less attractive kind. Off the sandy shores of Table Bay, amidst all the beauty, lies another place whose face has caused many in this land to weep. Robben Island – once a leper colony, and most notoriously during my lifetime the South African Alcatraz – an open cage that for many years imprisoned Nelson Mandela and other 'political dissidents' deemed to pose a danger to the state. Inevitably therefore, through all my memories and musings there runs this thread, this tension, this sad truth; that while Cape Town for some was a place of freedom and unsurpassed beauty, for others it housed a dictatorial regime and personified aching hardship, suffering, and terrifying brutality.

Mountains

the mountains on the mainland are no Cinderellas
today they blush fresh radiance
glowing with joyful adolescent faces uplifted to the 'maturing
    sun'
who touches their snow-white crowns like a celestial fairy
    godmother
transforming them into translucent gold
dripping liquid amber down furrowed sides
adorning their long and weathered forms
with robes fit for royalty

from a distant shore
these majestic figures appear so young and warm
inviting us to run and play
and shelter in the shadow of their strong and rising limbs

but for those drawing near
accepting the dare to scramble up their sides
breathe comes cold
expelled in clouds that hang silent in a quite indifferent air
and they listen when they're told not to linger long
nor overstay their welcome there

is there a truism here I wonder
as through this cottage pane I peer
and muse that warmth and beauty seldom are up close
what from a distance they once appeared to be

how quickly the mind springs to fantasy
on mountains rising over yonder sea

only to find after arriving breathlessly
that I'm still me despite the journey from there to here
and something far less grand
inhabits the land
than first caught and teased my eye

does that leave me scared to look
or cynical of what I see
by no means
I still am free
maybe a little wiser though
to recognize the childhood saying that
what's nice from far
sometimes is found to be
far from nice when applied
to everyday reality

so walk wary my dear friend
let feet be slow to up and go
where pleading eyes would tease and beg
for you to follow hastily
tread cautiously into the unknown
tomorrow and tomorrow
even though
'tis an infuriatingly petty pace

Elephant Graves

this mid-life journey
winds through surprising twists and turns

on one particular day it led me by way
of some hauntingly beautiful vistas
places where light melts luminous mellow
hints of raw sienna in the late noon sun
and the valley flows green
draped in heavy foliage dripping humid
beading rivulets from leaves and branches
into an insatiable earth

a place where thunder clouds loom large like a Constable
    canvas
swirling brushstrokes of purple black and gray
lightning bolts hurl large thunder claps at midday
with a drum-roll for the deluge that floods the plains and
    cools the heat
transforming dirt into a rich red mud that oozes soft
slither sliding alive under feet

this is the place
where the elephants come
and go to die

it's surprising
that these large creatures with hardly anything to fear
should display such sensitivity
and appear to grieve so deeply

when death draws near
and afflicts a member of their herd

when such a tragedy occurs
they hang around until the wounded or sick one has died
and even then their departure is neither swift nor easy
but rather ponderously slow
in thought and motion

I'm beginning to understand what those moments feel like
the sight and sound of elephants mourning
weaving 'round corpses
large ears flapping and slack trunks slapping the dirt
and kissing the dead
it all resonates with me right now
I muse
on furrowed brows wrinkled gray
framing dark wise eyes
under an African sun baking hot copper skies
that age the young in a day
and set fire to the tinder-dry plains across which
these Herculean warriors instinctively plod
their eternal somnambulistic trek
ponderously traversing this most ancient of lands

elephants grieving

it's an image portraying for me an excruciating meeting
of past and future in a painful present
lingering around the corpse of what once was
and hesitating unable to move on to what might be
alone with the knowledge
that something once dear is being left behind
decaying
dust to dust in the grave-ground of lost loves and fallen
    dreams
that bleach-boned valley

fertile with loss and pregnant with sad vulnerability
where turning in circles is routine
backwards and forwards pulls unseen
in a strange tug-of-war
facing the future and retreating from the past
following
feet shuffling
forward
yet still straining with eyes lagging slowly behind
to catch a last gasp or glimpse
of that which now lies in the embers of yesterday
but echoes on today painfully pulsating
within the confines of a beating heart
I have come to that poignant place
where my choices mean that some will die
and those who once shared flesh with me
here too will lie
I cannot stop myself circling
reluctant to leave
not wanting to stay
nudging the corpses
in anger I grieve
there'll be no resurrection here
nor hope of reprieve

slowly I begin the dizzy ascent
from this wretched valley floor
time alone will tell what has been left to die
what will live
and why

Thank God for Friends

thank God for those whose words became flesh
when broken in spirit I cursed the world
and sought empathic solitude with Job
for months on end
thank God for those few friends
whose love never did end at a prescribed boundary fence
nor did they withdraw because of
what they heard and saw in me
for quite some long and dreary time

again and again they worked miracles
as gently they moved through my walls of silence
and walked across my turmoiled waters of despair
stilling the storm by staying near
speaking comfort to my fear
and peace to the anger that beat me into corners
and pummeled me with taunting admonitions

it's hard to clench my fist
when someone holds my hand
and sensitively listens to understand
at least to some degree
the emotion-ravaged wilderness where I have been of late
dragging my heels in slow and heavy steps
where words stutter and fail to translate
in any sensible way
the unbelievably bleak despair
and utter dismay within

thank God for those whose words made flesh
never let me down nor abandoned me to drown
in that sea through which I furiously thrashed
instead they stayed
and with grains of faith gathered from their hidden store
they prayed and coaxed me quietly back to shore
and warmed my shivering being with blankets of love
until the blood began to flow once more

Yvonne (My Mother)

My mother had jet-black hair that curled on her shoulders in the style of the day – late 50's - early 60's. She wore red lipstick and painted her toenails and fingernails red as well. She was quiet and undemonstrative and never appeared to me to be very happy. I'm not sure what she did with her time and I don't know what interested her or what she enjoyed. She didn't come out with us when we went walking on the mountain or swimming at the beach. Yvonne was her name – I called her mum or ma – she remains quite a mystery to me.

When I was about ten years old we had a dog named Dopey, and he had the bad habit of chasing cars and snapping at their wheels as they rolled down the road next to our house. One day while my brother and I were playing 'cricket' in the road Dopey chased a car that snapped back and he was killed. I can still see Dopey trotting slowly back to my feet where he lay down to take his last breath. My mother told me that it was ok to cry; I was stoic even then and was surprised to see her shed a tear.

She called me 'darling' one afternoon while she was having tea with Judy, a friend of hers – I remember liking how it felt.

In the last years of her life our home was full of tension. My brother had cancer and endured some major operations (which he miraculously survived) and my mother seemed to cry a lot, leave the table upset, and occasionally raise her voice at my father after we had gone to bed. I remember lying in bed and listening, the tension tightening my body like a corkscrew. No one ever kissed, hugged, held, or affirmed very much – at least not in the memories I can recall.

I remember asking her to play cards one night. She stood at the hall table and said, "When I come out of hospital we'll all play together."

I thought, "You won't be coming home from the hospital."

A few days later she went into the local hospital for treatment and died the following week from complications. The telephone rang just before we went to school and my father answered and left in a hurry, saying nothing much. I went into my brother's room and told him that I thought mum had died. "Rubbish" he replied.

Midway through school that morning the headmaster called me out of my classroom and told me that my father would be picking my brother and me up from school at twelve. Returning to my desk I was asked by the master what that was all about. "I think it's something to do with my mother who is sick in hospital, sir," I replied. How can you say that you think your mother has died?

My brother and I climbed into the car.... "Mum's died, hasn't she?" I said.

"How did you know? Yes, she died this morning in her sleep...."

Dad took us all to the beach that afternoon. I swam and sat on the sand surveying other people there; I wanted to say, "Do you know that my mother died this morning?" Everything seemed so normal and unaffected. A part of me surprisingly experienced relief – now the tension and fighting would end. Some years later the hole she left behind became more apparent – and I grieved her passing without talking to anyone.

I was not present at my mother's funeral. Instead my brother and I accompanied well-meaning friends to water-ski in a large dam outside Clanwilliam (a rural town about four hours outside of Cape Town). My father hardly ever talked about her and never admitted to any problems in the marriage (except in the privacy of his diaries, which I read after his death thirty years later). I don't recall many conversations that helped us process her life or her death. She just slipped away in April, 1965 – when I was 12 – and never returned home to play cards.

The following year, on the anniversary of her death, Gill, my older sister and I walked down the road to St. Thomas church to attend an early-morning communion service. We were alone with the elderly priest who was presiding over the service that morning and he gave thanks for my mother's life during the prayers. That was a pattern, it seems to me; sharing grief in quiet and looking stoic, and receiving some form of comfort in the midst of strangers rather than within my family. It was probably the most intimate moment I have ever shared with Gill. I'd almost forgotten about that morning until I started recording these memories.

We Are Like Oceans

we are like oceans

yesterday
wild waters restless in motion

today
a brooding tranquil and quiet sea

tomorrow
who knows how high the swells will rise and fall

we are like oceans

shores and waves on sandy beaches
rocks with ripping tides and gentle swells
whose depths hide murky secrets
camouflaged amidst coral-encrusted folds
way down in a cold below

we are like oceans

on the surface light plays innocently in the shallows
and water lisps rhythmic songs to the music
of rolling pebbles brushing sands and tumbling shells
cascading sounds that sooth the soul
warmed by the summer sun

we are like oceans

whose first appearance is not all there is to know
we change and breathe with every ebb and flow of an ocean
    tide
pulled tugged and again let go by a thousand lunar threads
our waters caress the shores of countless friendly
smooth and sandy places
then pound and beat with breaking waves against strange rigid
    cliffs
whose unyielding faces stand stern before our wet
    tempestuousness

we are like oceans

mysterious and frightening
beautiful and dangerous
life-giving yet deadly when awakened or aroused
it all depends on how you find us
and our mood at the time

many will sail swim or dive in our domain
some will delight in what they find
while others will settle on different shores

Servants

During the late 1950's, our family moved into my grandmother's large house, Penrose, situated on the lower slopes of Devil's Peak in the suburb of Rosebank. It was a double-story Victorian home with a wrought-iron verandah, many rooms with high ceilings and a large garden that I loved to explore.

However, most significant was the fact that for the first time in my life Black servants were employed to work in our house. The women who worked were called maids; they wore uniforms and aprons and did all the housework, the cooking, cleaning, laundry, ironing, and child-care. I am struck with the realization that my memories of this period have more to do with my relationships with the servants than with my parents. My mother did not work, and yet I have few memories of participating in many activities with her.

I remember coming home from school and sitting in the kitchen at the big scrubbed wooden table and talking to Lizzie while she split peas from their pods and prepared the evening meal. She was a large, slightly dishevelled lady, probably in her fifties, who used to sing softly to herself in a breathy wheezy kind of way. I would chat across the table and try and help and felt very at home with her. On Wednesdays she would clean the silver, and the smell of 'Silvo' filled the kitchen on those days. Knives, forks, spoons, and other tableware would be rubbed with the Silvo and then when caked white and dry rubbing with a clean cloth would magically restore them to a sparkling shine.

Godfrey was the gardener who came to work once a week. I enjoyed scratching around in the dirt while he weeded. He was an older man with a gentle way with children and he always had time for me – I loved the cocktail odor of sweat, earth and tobacco that accompanied him wherever he went. His voice was deep and rough like a gravel road and as was the custom of the time he addressed me as 'Master John'.

Lenie was employed as our nanny and she took care of the children for about seven years. She was short, slightly plump, with long black hair that used to be curled up into a bun when she wore her maid's uniform. Lenie took us for walks around the block with Punchy the dog. Sometimes we went to play in the park. My favourite walk was down to the Pepsi-Cola bottling factory. We would stand on the sidewalk and peer through the large factory window and watch the bottles jiggling along their conveyer belt. They bumped and shook in single file as they made their way to the 'bottle-cap machine' where metal lids were firmly pressed on slender necks and their delicious contents sealed ready for distribution.

Like many middle-class White children in South Africa in the late 50's I had very little idea about Black people being oppressed and about the real meaning of apartheid. I don't recall seeing them as servants so much as companions, and I was too young to reflect on what happened to their families while they toiled in our house and looked after the likes of me. I didn't question whether they were content living in a single room at the back of our house and apart from their families. I couldn't really imagine them as mothers and wives – they were our servants.

But I was no paragon of virtue either and the most shameful incident I can recall is when I was entertaining a friend at home after school. Ralph and I wanted to go somewhere and Lenie would not allow us to do so; I was indignant and to impress Ralph swore at Lenie with all the words I had ever heard or could imagine. I was probably ten years old at the time. That evening my father spoke to me very sternly and made me apologize to Lenie for being so rude. Inwardly I was still indignant that she should have spoken to my father and betrayed me; how could a ten-year-old develop such arrogance and 'attitude' toward a woman in her mid-thirties? It is frightening how insidiously the weeds of prejudice grow in fertile minds and lives when the garden is not well tended to prevent deep roots from being set.

Samaritan

it's a
'long and winding road'
from
Jerusalem to Jericho
shimmering in the hot desert air
piano-hinged to rock and sand
precariously suspended between
mountain peak and valley deep
heaven and hell
so to speak

sometime
somewhere
along this lonely path
the robbers fell
ambushing a travelling Jew
to beat rob and discard him
bleeding among the rocks
home of snakes and scorpion lairs
could've been me or could've been you
abandoned there

alone he lay
between peak and floor
for a very long time
strong enough to bleed
but too weak to speak
coughing and groaning
moaning in God's dusty land

and all the while
fellow travellers trod by
religiously keeping their pledge
they veered wide to the other side
hugging the mountain
steering clear of the edge
too busy too holy
too clean to get dirty
too righteous
too proud
too stuck up to bend down
could've been me or could've been you
walking by

at last someone stopped and stooped
to wash the wounds and bind the sores
of the half-dead wretch whom they never knew
and certainly to whom no favour from them was due
furthermore the one who knelt to care
wasn't one of the chosen few
not even of the tribe of the dying Jew

he was 'only' a Samaritan
beliefs not quite right
rejected and despised
shoved out of sight
one who knew the bleeding place well
for like the man in the dust before him
the Samaritan also
harboured wounds that bled profusely inside
he was familiar with his tribe's steep and rocky road
cruelly carved
relentlessly and religiously unraveled
down through the mountains and valleys of history's timeless
    trails
no fault of this Samaritan for his ancestor's tales

nevertheless he was the one whom Jesus chose
to be the hands that staunched the flow
of sorrow and pain from that poor undignified man

he was the one whom Jesus chose
to be the hero of sermon's and Sunday schools
for generations to come
traversing highways
spanning countless cultures oceans and lands
illustrating God's love manifest through a humble servant's
      heart
extending healing hands to all the helpless thief-stricken Jews
scattered in the ragged Diaspora of human tribes
throughout a raped and ravaged Eden

He always knew that pointed fingers
and spotless hands never rescued anyone
nor drew them to safety
nor snatched them
from the trampling feet of harm's way

and before the compassionate Samaritan
there was Moses
Hosea
David and Jeremiah
Ruth and Sarah

and after him came
Lydia
and Mary
and Mary
Saul and Peter
and many many more
all who'd tasted the dust of a valley floor
and in wounded despair
felt a Samaritan's touch on matted hair
fingers graced with a love

that seemed too good to be true
at the time

'twas humble love that raised them
from their sorry ground to donkey's back and then to bed
until at last they walked again toward new and loftier peaks

only then did they dare speak

and now their words
embellished with their deeds
give life to other frail flesh
too wounded and too weak
to know how to ask for help....
or who it is they really seek

Mercy

we've written tunes
and sung songs of Christ and love
and compassion for all
for God knows how long

yet still....
our lives together struggle to reflect
the meaning of the sound
and those ideals that flood our hearts
sincerely overflowing through our mouths
into the lives of one another

yet still....
in the quiet of our inner selves the same words haunt
as we grapple to bridge the gap within
between theory and practical application

therefore when someone admits to struggle
we resonate and nod
we are encouraged and don't feel quite so alone

yet still....
we are mere mortals
frightened by our propensity for sin
especially if we're spiritual

mercy is not our natural or even supernatural response
to the revelation of that capacity to fall within another
whom we call friend

yet still....
it's to that end we're ultimately called
to impart grace and mercy
rather than judgement

for now we untruly see through veiled glass and frosted lens
and there is no clarity in our vision
nor maturity in our comprehension of ourselves
never mind of one another

yet still....
humility is born again and again
in stables found in countless human forms
where Jesus lives 'mong cows and men

God's creative reality filled with ambiguity
a mystery in the twilight zones

yet still....
life here
is always becoming
and not yet being

Reflections

what do you think will happen when the wind dies
and the waves cease their chopping
and the restless waters settle to velvet
and with silky calm caress your delicate skin

that's when the deep stirs and whispers words
at last free to rise from the tranquil quiet buried within
like little bubbles popping up to the surface

and peering down
a mirrored frown squints back
as face to face we approach a place
of shimmering reflection
introspection and contemplation
a realm seldom visited by you and me
and usually suppressed beneath
the rolling waves of things to do

but there is no need to fear
here
where two strangers timidly draw near
peering over the edge
reaching up and reaching down
perhaps to befriend maybe even to mend
the rift that persists between the two

it's like diving into a raging sea

and piercing through that fierce wet outer layer
discovering another world

not near as grim as was imagined from afar
a world that sways languorously in gentle swells
where creatures live and coral breathes
where life is born
and beauty lies in myriad forms
like oyster pearls rainbow fish and turtle shells
and from the depths the divers rise
bearing dripping treasure
to surprise with unexpected pleasure
those who on the surface dwell

Mining Deep

mining is dirty work
men with lamp-lit helmets
disappear underground
riding rattling cages
sliding down steep shafts of steel tracks
that burrow through twisted miles of subterranean tunnels
feverishly clawed scraped
and shaped by their own hands

men sweat
working dust and dirt
blasting and jack-hammering the coalface
coughing and cursing
relentlessly fracturing the earth
loading fragment after fragment onto trolleys
that haul the mother lode to the surface
for money and profit
wages and food

at long shift's end like moths to light
with blackened masks and battered boxes
the men scurry home
and return clean in the morning
to grumble and curse as they
burrow deeper into the rich dirt

there's all kinds of mining

diamonds coal copper gold
zinc uranium

iron ore and much more buried deep
for treasure seldom lies at the feet
of those who walk on easy street
and then there's mining for words
which is where I explore
traveling below the surface
down the shaft of human being
into the dust and bedrock of emotions and feelings
often buried under time and the grime of years
of neglect

it's a mine of joy and peace
frequently hidden deep under pain and sorrow
where trauma lies and questions grow
ancient longings protrude from the rubble
discarded broken bones
evidence of what might have been
of what once was or was cut short
and perished way too young

I burrow chip and chisel into the human underground
seeking priceless words filled with meaning
to bring to the surface
buried hopes and forgotten jewels
that for too long now have lain discarded and ignored

the words of greatest value
lie in the depths no eye perceives
but only a tender beating heart
hears and feels and intuitively discerns
their invisible presence
unattended they evaporate
fly away or die
they are simple gold
most exquisite when unrefined
priceless only as shared and told
from heart to heart and deep to deep

many are miners few are finders
parents and children
husbands and wives
brothers and sisters
friends, peers, and lovers
with trembling hands they touch and marvel
drinking deep the words lost and now found
when uttered above the ground
is there any more beautiful a sound than
"I love you."

A Short Story....

The origin of this tale is either in the African or Native Indian tradition and describes an initiation event for boys on the path to becoming men. One of the rituals required a boy to stay alone by himself in the forest all night.

A father would escort his son into the forest outside their camp or village as the sun melted behind the hills. He would select a suitable place for the initiation event where his son was to remain for the night. If the boy cried or walked away he would fail the test. The last thing the boy saw in the fading light was his father disappearing into the dusk, leaving him entirely alone.

Imagine the experience for a young lad who would not have been older than twelve years of age; the strange sounds, the howl of a wolf, fear amplified by a vivid imagination magnified every rustle, and there was always the possibility of real danger lurking in the form of a hungry and wild animal. All night the boy had to wrestle alone to overcome his fear and weariness in order that he might prove he was indeed worthy of receiving the coveted mantle of manhood.

At last the dawn began to break and slowly the darkness faded. The boy would obviously be relieved as he began to discern the shapes of the trees and bushes emerging all around him. Then to his astonishment he saw his father standing very close to where he himself had been all night long. His father was armed with weapons and no doubt smiled as their eyes met for the first time. It was at that moment the boy would realize that his father had been standing there with him all the time. His father had not walked away after all. He had loved his son enough to allow him to be tested, while at the same time making sure that he was protected from harm. The boy had never been alone or unattended for even one minute.

God promises that He will never leave us or abandon us. In my darkest hours, and at many other times in my life, belief in His faithfulness has been all that I have been able to hold on to. The belief that God would be there for me even when I did not feel or experience anything but my own despair, anger and sense of abandonment. I have quite simply had to trust that His faithfulness and His promises and love would protect me, even at times from myself.

The dawn has broken after the longest darkest night I could ever have imagined. I can discern the shapes around me and He has been true to His word. That truth moves me to tears, for I am not abandoned after all – He has been standing there all the time. And He is there for you as well, because He does not play favourites and He's not afraid of the dark.

Deep Calls to Deep

deep calls to deep
even within depression's coma
and the long nightmarish sleep

a memory stirs the heart
a twitch of life inside
of what once was
a pulse that quickens
and quietly brings to rebirth
a spirit that years ago
dragged itself bleeding
into the shadows to die
to kill the pain

deep calls to deep
and does not cease
nor withdraw
just because I am weak
and fail to speak or stand firm
my soul thirsts for God
for the living God

now at last
the life that slowly ebbed away
seeps into my tidal pool
once more

Please God

please God
can I go now
I've been in this corner
for an eternity
saying I'm sorry to the wall
and reflecting on all
the consequences
in fact it's been so long
I've forgotten how
to turn around
and re-enter life
where once for me
joy did abound

please God
may I go now
and begin again
even though we both know
that nothing will ever be the same
in my disfigured Eden
misshapen now perhaps
but somehow still a place
I'd like to explore
and learn more of me and You
and the meaning of it all

please God
may I leave now
but not alone
and may I have my heart back

and will You
can I
how do I
dare to risk
and believe
and give myself
I feel like a newborn
but not so pure and innocent

please God
do You think
I could be born again
and we could try once more
I'm scared
of You
and them
and me
and the anger inside
and all the voices

please God
help me be
again

Summer Evening

God cut His finger last night
and the sky bled red
all the way down to a lazy sea
splashing ripples
across the pebbled sand to
quick-sink beneath below

distant mountains leaned ink-black
against an exquisitely wounded heaven
where fragments of clouds stretched torn-ragged
and stained by the spreading fire through which
vapour trails corkscrewed their disintegrating paths
into a fading horizon

we stood along the shore wide-eyed with awe
and I wondered what such beauty
stirred in other strangers lingering there

but then again when God bleeds
people tend to stop and stare

Creativity

have you ever seen creativity grow
would you know where to look
and looking
would you know what to do
and how to be with what you saw
when you did see

it takes a keen eye and a sensitive spirit
to spy the first shy blade
peering gingerly upward and outward
squinting into the light from the hidden
place where the seed is formed
in the human underground

more often than not we'll unwittingly find
the remnants of innocence
and a hope that once danced
to the rhythm of an excited heartbeat
the footprints of a joyful vulnerability
and a playful idealism that dared to risk and be exposed

but in the hollow void that love and affirmation left behind
silence and ignorance parented dumb and blind
a malnourished creativity
that gasped for air and strength to breath
orphaned and unattended
it stood alone
ignored
or worse still
scorned

in such a place no young life can keep a steady pace
instead it withers upon its fragile stem
bends its face in humiliated disgrace
and droops and dies before the buds are fully formed
and what once was or even might have been
falls quietly unseen
to maybe nourish the dream of another still to come
a child perhaps of this disillusioned one

it takes a green thumb to harvest creative fruit
full-grown
ripe and mature
for it is surely more than sun and moisture
that nourishes a fragile plant to blossom

creative care buds from roots
within the gardener's soul
discerning a flower in full bloom
while others wander ever blind
to the seed cradled in fetal form
within creation's fertile womb
and sometimes with hasty plucking
busy hands and tidy minds
rip tender shoots from the soil
roots and all
and seeing no need
discard them as yet more pesky weed

but all is not lost
for even when tossed aside
to lie in shriveled
expressionless paralysis
still the ember will not die
nor such a seed be killed

I'm Still Not There Yet

I'm still not there yet

caught
paralyzed
sinking into quicksand
sucked down by despair
gasping for air
grabbing for straws
snatching for hope....

I'm still not there now

dancing on streets paved with gold
radiant with joy
laughing through music-filled days
where sorrow is healed
and every tear at last
at last is wiped away

I'm somewhere in-between
and it's here we have met
and spent some time
you and I
so incomplete

light has crested the hill
and the valley
though still dim
is brighter now
hope

mysterious as the dew in the country dawn
has been restored

behold all things will be made new....
may it indeed be so

Behold, I Make All Things New....

It is early spring, March 2003, as I complete these manuscripts and edit them for the last time. Almost 7 years have passed since the first rumblings began; I would never have dreamed how long and slow a process lay ahead. The healing is still not complete and I do not have a fairytale ending, but there's a lot more light than darkness now.

Over the past months the land has been cleared around the cabin I am renovating and the trees have been thinned to allow more sunlight to shine in. The work has been symbolic for me of new beginnings, new strength, new hope, and new resolve in the midst of incompleteness. Recycling and recreation have been part of the cycle of life on earth from the very beginning, and it is God's gift to every person as well.

I'm reminded of an occasion when God seemed to quietly speak to me 25 years ago (I hate it when people say 'God told me'). I was a theological student in Oxford, somewhat reluctantly attending a joint evening service with another college. My lack of enthusiasm was mainly due to the style and format of the celebration. It followed the 'high church' Anglican tradition incorporating robes, bells, incense, and an austere formality in a ritual I never fully appreciated. Be that as it may, we dutifully gathered in the historic church in suburban Oxford for the service to commence.

I had been discouraged by the lack of change in my life and was wondering how God could keep forgiving the same old things again and again, and why bother anyway? These thoughts were mulling around in my head and heart as I sat in the church, where I did not want to be. Then like a slow awakening and stirring within I believe God began to speak, or at least whisper to me quite unexpectedly. He revealed a truth that changed the whole evening for me and has been a source of hope and inspiration ever since.

A few evenings earlier BBC TV had aired a news clip reporting how the Royal Air Force had used two old ships that they had towed out into the English Channel for bombing practice. The ships were strategically positioned in deep water and deliberately sunk. This was the image that God used to illustrate His point. The 'Divine action replay' began with my standing beside Jesus on the cliffs of Dover surveying the Channel. He pointed in the distance to the two ships floating on the water, useless hulls potentially dangerous to other shipping if they had been abandoned there.

We stood silently and watched the aircraft fly overhead and drop their bombs. At first there appeared to be no effect, then one ship listed and the other began to lift her prow high as the ocean poured into the stern. Before long both vessels had disappeared beneath the surface, leaving behind no trace of their presence except an empty ocean and the waves rolling as if nothing had happened.

Jesus spoke first, "John, how long are you going to stand here and wait for those ships to return to the surface?"

"They can't come back up," I replied, "I've just watched them being sunk, it's impossible."

"If you had just arrived here now and looked out, you would never have known those ships had been there at all, would you? Let's go to the bottom of the ocean, and see what's happened to them." Jesus smiled, obviously enjoying the moment.

In a flash we did just that, such is the miracle of the mind and spirit. When I saw the ships again they were no longer dangerous floating chunks of iron. Now, on the ocean floor they had been transformed into reefs teeming with an astounding variety of sea life. Fish swam and darted everywhere with coral and barnacles and other forms of plants sprouting from every inch of the vessels' surface.

Jesus spoke again. "John, when you give Me something, or ask Me for forgiveness, I want you to know that I take whatever you give Me as surely and completely as these ships sank into the ocean today. Whatever you entrust to Me is taken forever and will never surface again in My memory, nor should they arise as doubts in your heart and mind either.

"Take note of what has happened because this is also about transformation. When those ships sank they filled with water and they sank into water. In other words, the water and the ships became one – ocean in the ship and the ship in the ocean. The result was something wonderful took place, a miracle happened. What had become useless and dangerous was transformed into a reef providing shelter and life for many other creatures to thrive in.

"Why am I telling you this?" Jesus asked. "Because I want you to know that I can take all the negative, and all the mistakes and rebellion in your life and recycle them into new life-giving gifts that will bless you and those around you. If you entrust them to Me I'll perform that miracle every time. I can transform anything that is ugly, dangerous, useless, and poisonous, into something beautiful and enriching for you and for others."

I recount this 'reflection' because I do believe that eventually anything and everything in our lives can be used for good, even the awfulness of depression with all the flotsam and jetsam surrounding that trauma. In my experience the 'religious' people have a far greater struggle judging others than I think God ever has.

The apostle Paul announced with deep conviction that he was the greatest of all sinners. Indeed he had been guilty of authorizing the death and persecution of some of the early Christians. But God met him on the Damascus Road and transformed him into one of the most astute and gifted writers and Christian apologists the world has ever known.

Enduring a life-threatening depression with all the reasons and circumstances leading up to that cataclysmic event under public scrutiny, particularly as a Christian leader, has not left me with much dignity or pride intact. There is no longer any reputation to worry about or ego to try and defend (which is strangely liberating actually), just an acknowledgement of human weakness entrusted to God to recycle. Now I'm just an old wreck in the ocean waiting for the coral to grow and the fish to arrive; all I have to do is rest on the sand and let it happen ... and I can laugh and smile again!

God's Slipstream

through all these turbulent times
there are a few truths
that I have begun to learn

that authentic peace
purely distilled
is only found in the slipstream of the Lord

I have learned
that although God 'has seen it all'
He is not indifferent to me
despite my feelings that
He has appeared to be exceedingly disinterested
at times when I felt I needed Him the most

I have learned
that there remains much I do not comprehend
but I would rather
entrust these unanswered questions
into His hands
than clutch them uselessly
within the feeble wrapping of my intellect
for the maggots of bitterness to devour

I have learned that whether
I move in or out of God's slipstream
His love is deeper than the darkest depths of my despair
and His mercy is greater than is my ability to rebel
and that despite all my running
I have never leaped a boundary fence

into a field beyond His reach
or trodden a path that was a new frontier for Him
I have learned
that His grace is more solid than is my wavering faith
and that His faithfulness is unconditional and forever

I have learned again that God is the source
of all my truth, all of my hope, all of my healing,
all my present and all of my future

I have learned to keep learning (like Paul)
how to be content in every circumstance
and that contentment will surely be found
while living ever so imperfectly
within the slipstream of the Lord
all of my days

and I have learned
that it is still easier
to write these words
than to live this life
which is why
I need others
and they need me

Over 3,000 years ago Moses first uttered the original rendition of this prayer, that I put to music some years back. I've always found it to be a powerful and meaningful 'blessing' extending the love and mercy of God to others, including you right now.

the Lord bless you
and keep you
and make His face shine upon you
and be gracious to you
the Lord turn His face toward you
and give you His peace